4.99

Ethics

In Business Now Series
Ethics Francis P. McHugh
Graphs and Charts Renée Huggett
Markets Renée Huggett
Retailing Peter Jones and Steve Baron

IN BUSINESS NOW

Ethics

Francis P. McHugh

MACMILLAN

First published 1991 by
THE MACMILLAN PRESS LTD
Houndmills, Basingstoke, Hampshire RG21 2XS
and London
Companies and representatives
throughout the world

ISBN 0–333–54446–3

A catalogue record for this book is available
from the British Library.

Printed in Hong Kong

10   9   8   7   6   5   4   3   2
00 99 98 97 96 95 94 93 92

Contents

Contents

Acknowledgements

The author wishes to thank Ruth Maskery for invaluable help with research in the preparation of this book.

The support and encouragement of Von Hugel Institute, St Edmund's College, Cambridge, and Christian Social Ethics Research Unit are also gratefully acknowledged.

The author and publishers wish to thank the following who have kindly given permission for the use of copyright material.

The Advertising Standards Authority Ltd for material sourced to their publications;
Barclays Bank plc for their logo;
Birds Eye Wall's Ltd for advertising material;
Collins Publishers for a figure from *Credit and Debt; Sorting it Out* by Schluter and Lee, Marshall Pickering, 1989;
Corning Ltd, on behalf of Grey Ltd, for advertising material;
Corporate Communication Strategy for figure 'Take up of shares in all-employee share schemes';
ECOTEC Research and Consulting Ltd for figure, 'Gross annual cost of pollution control by private sector industry 1988';
The Controller of Her Majesty's Stationery Office for Crown copyright material;
Hobsons Publishing plc for figure from *Finding Out . . . About the City*, 1989; Holden Meehan for table, 'Investment with Conscience';
Jubilee Centre Publications Ltd for data from the Jubilee Centre Debt Study Survey;
Charles Letts & Co. Ltd for material from *Business Studies* by David Floyd, 1989;
ICI for their Satinwood advertising material;
Lloyds Bank for their logo;
McGraw-Hill Inc. for table from *Business and Society* by K. Davis and W. Frederick, 5th edition, 1984;
Midland Bank for their logo;
Monks Partnership Ltd for data on highly paid directors' salaries;
National Westminster Bank PLC for their logo;
Nationwide Anglia Building Society for their logo;
The Observer Ltd, for adapted tables 'Fatalities at work' and 'Construction: the most dangerous trade', *The Observer*, 6th May 1990;
Times Newspapers Ltd for table on fraud, *MORI/The Sunday Times*, October, 1985.

Every effort has been made to trace all copyright holders, but if any have been inadvertently overlooked the publishers will be pleased to make the necessary arrangement at the first opportunity.

Unit 1 | What Business Ethics is about

Introduction

Business is about buying and selling goods and services, like Nike sport shoes, compact discs, transport, banking and leisure facilities. Business is about making money, about profit and success. Some people would say that it is about these three things only, and make the following typical statements about business:

- it's a jungle out there;
- as long as you are not caught you can do what you like;
- most people cheat in business;
- nobody ever got rich through being honest;
- greed is good;
- everybody else does it, so it must be all right for me too.

These statements paint too black a picture. They give the impression that all business is conducted in this way. But the truth is that business is both bad and good. As with everything else in life, there is right and wrong in business.

Business ethics is about rights and wrongs in the world of business. For example, you have left a tracksuit and three shirts at the dry cleaners, and when you collect them the young assistant makes a mistake and charges you for the tracksuit but for only two shirts. You notice the mistake, but you do not tell her. That is dishonest. Business ethics says you should tell her: business ethics is about **honesty**. Or, a family is going abroad and decide to let their flat. They promise it to a young couple, but while they are away getting references and the deposit, an attractive young woman turns up and offers £20 a month extra. The husband accepts this offer. Business ethics says he should have kept his word: it is about **trust**. Or, you are a salesman for a firm which sells a chemical cleaner. You read in a 'Friends of the Earth' leaflet that this particular cleaner is damaging to health and harmful to the environment. Business ethics is about **respect** for creation and says that you have a responsibility to do something in the circumstances. Lastly, it has been reported that a Regional Health Authority has told a Local Health Authority to delay paying bills until the next financial year, in an attempt to reduce spending in the current year. If the report is correct, then this advice is unfair to small businesses with

1

cash flow problems. Business ethics is about **fairness**, and would question the advice given.

So, business ethics is about **honesty**, **trust**, **respect** and **fairness** in all business dealings.

1 The real world

Take a walk around your town. Its industrial, commercial and business activity meets the needs and wants of the people in the area and, through trading and exports, of people in other areas and overseas. Business provides for both needs and wants, and there is a difference between them. 'Needs' refers to those things which are necessary for survival, like food, clothing and warmth. 'Wants' are desires for extras, like refrigerators or holidays, which are not necessary, but which do help to make life more enjoyable.

Figure 1
Human needs are limited

Figure 2
*Human wants are
unlimited*

The High Street is always busy. That is where most of the shopping is done. When you go into the supermarket to buy a packet of biscuits you are faced with a problem of choice, for there are four shelves of biscuits with 136 different brands. The packets are nearly all the same weight, but the prices range from 49p to 99p. You begin to wonder how prices are fixed and if they are *fair*. As you wait at the check-out desk to pay 57p for your packet of chocolate biscuits, you notice the customer in front of you slipping a tin of polish into her bag without putting it on the counter to be checked. For the individual who is cheating there is the question of *dishonesty*; and for you there is the problem of whether you should say anything.

The District Council offices are in West Street, where local government people deal with the business of collecting the refuse, maintaining the street lighting, public toilets, parks, recreation centres and many other services. These are partly paid for by the Community Charge or Poll Tax, which is higher than the former rates bill for many people. There is a problem about the ability of some to pay, as can be seen from the protest outside the Town Hall on the day the Poll Tax was fixed. A few people shattered the windows of the Town Hall. There is one ethical problem here about *fairness* and another about *respect* for property.

Further along West Street is the Sixth Form College, which is paid for partly by Community Charge, partly by Uniform Business Rate and partly by Central Government support. It is important to remember, when it comes to discussions about fairness in paying for local services, that it takes more than the Poll Tax to pay for them. Local businesses pay part of the bill (this is called the Uniform Business Rate); and Central Government pays more than either Local Government or businesses. Apart from educating and training young people, the college also provides employment for teachers, caretakers, kitchen staff and cleaners. Some of the cleaners (mostly women) are part-time workers who have no contracts of employment and, consequently, fewer rights than other groups of workers. Because they work for less than 17 hours per week for the employer, the law treats part-time workers like casual labour, and they do not have contracts to defend their jobs and conditions of employment. The Trade Union has been discussing the *unfairness* of treatment accorded to women; and everyone has been discussing the lack of *respect* for property in those who stoned the Town Hall.

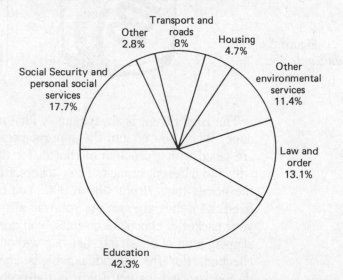

Figure 3
Local authority
expenditure

There are a number of important businesses in the Town Square, including building societies, banks and insurance companies. They conduct much of the financial business in the town and could not operate if there was no *trust* in their agreement to honour their word. The electricity board, the gas board and British Telecom are also sited in the Town Square. Until recently they were in public ownership (that is, legally held by Government on behalf of the people), but they have been sold off as private companies (that is, 'privatised') and many local people bought shares in them. Again, the dealing in stocks and shares was based on *trust*, since the people who bought shares trusted the Government to ensure that shares were set at a fair price.

On the corner of North Street is the Oxfam shop, selling second-hand articles and hand-made goods produced by people in the Third World to raise money for the less fortunate people abroad. Ethics also directs us to look beyond our own town to honesty, trust, respect and fairness towards others in distant lands.

Activity

Copy out the following table and name four basic ethical or moral ideals. Give examples of how they may occur in everyday life.

Ethical ideals	Examples of how they apply
1.	
2.	
3.	
4.	

2 No simple solutions

The problem with ethical ideals or values such as honesty, trust, respect and fairness is that they are general and vague. Many business ethics statements are like this. A firm may have a number of different objectives which are not easy to reconcile. For example, a first objective might be that "the directors have an obligation to themselves and to the shareholders to maximise profit;" and a second objective might be that "the company has a responsibility to the community in which it operates, and to care for the wider environment." Paying for the second objective may cut back the profits required by the first objective.

Activity

Choose a well-known local firm and imagine (or, if you prefer, try to find out) the conflicts it might have.

Business ethics is a debating chamber of conflicting claims. It is about health, stress and safety at work. If one of your workers is drinking heavily, do you sack him even if his wife and family will suffer? Business ethics is about equality of opportunity at work; it is about sexual harassment at work, which one US company estimated recently cost it $7 million dollars in absenteeism and loss of workers; it is about keeping in touch with the community and, for example, helping the local colleges and schools. It is about older workers, retirement and making sure that pensions are fair. The great business enterprises of our day sometimes establish conventional beliefs to persuade people (they tend to call them 'consumers') to buy their products in order to maximise their profits. The conventional belief may be, for example, that mineral water is healthier than tap water. Salesmen are expected to push this conventional line, which the firm considers its 'truth'. The reality may be different, as may be judged from the temporary withdrawal of Perrier water in 1990, when it was said to contain health-endangering elements. The rights of the individual and the purposes and needs of the institution can easily be in tension.

Activity

Examine advertisements on TV and in magazines, and list some conventional beliefs that are being pushed by large institutions in order to sell their products. Explain how this approach can influence the consumer. For example, the ideal woman in adverts is alway slim: could this influence the teenage anorexic?

3   Two conflicting opinions

Some companies work on the assumption that their overriding duty is to make profits, and everything else takes second place to this. The famous US economist, Milton Friedman, put this view briefly:

"The one and only social responsibility of business is to increase profits."

Not everyone agrees with this. Dayton Hudson, the US drapery goods chain, tripled its sales and profits in a decade, but on different grounds from that advanced by Friedman:

"The business of business is serving society, not just making money . . . Profit is our reward for serving society well. Indeed, profit is the means and the measure of our service – but not an end in itself."

Profit is not a dirty word. There is no development, growth, investment or expansion without it. But the profit motive in itself cannot resolve business tensions and conflicts. The basic principle of business ethics is: 'People matter; persons are more important than things; treat others as you would have them treat you'.

Dilemma

Levi-Strauss, the maker of jeans and denims, was taken over by the Hans family and turned into a private company. It claimed a strong ethical basis. The new owners discovered that a top manager, in an attempt to maximise profits, had ended up with a sweatshop atmosphere which they considered wrong. Should they:

1. Sacrifice his high productivity and profit and sack him?
2. Keep him on, but distribute part of the profits to the workers?
3. Get him to modify the pressure he is putting on the workers?

Activity

Look in newspapers and glossy magazines for words like 'perfect' and 'basic', which make buying attractive, but are describing a make-believe world. Explain whether you think this is right or wrong, and why.

List of words   Your explanation

....

....

....

....

....

Figure 4

Unit 2 | A Fair Deal

1 The real world

In order to find out what inspires business people in their work, what their values are and whether questions of ethics (that is, about good and bad, right and wrong) influence their business activity, a survey of managers was conducted on an industrial estate in Surrey. Out of 130 firms on the estate, 37 were selected for detailed analysis. Answers to some of the questions are summarised below:

Number of employees	Motivation	Business ethics (BE)	Internal environment	Community involvement
5–10	Profit; making a living; survival	Conscience; vague idea of BE	Stress; no welfare	None
11–100	Profit; money; job satisfaction; market leadership	Ethical codes used; conscience	Stress; low welfare	None
100–200+	Profit; expansion; service to others; success	Most accepted a code; few accepted BE	Stress; low welfare provision	Half said none; some support for youth projects

From: *Worlds Apart: a report on Church and Industry on the Yorktown Industrial Estate, Surrey,* SNEHIM, Guildford, 1987.

Here are some conclusions from the survey:

- Most of the companies interviewed were motivated by profit and money.
- Success, survival, job-satisfaction, efficiency and service to others were also mentioned.
- There was little coherent response to questions on business ethics.

8

Activity

Using the headings in the table above, write a summary for a firm which is highly involved in business ethics.

2 Economics and business

Keywords in the table above which business people used to describe their work are: **profit-making, money, market leadership, expansion, success** and **service**. These are all positive and dynamic words, which serve as a good introduction to examining the meaning of economics and business. Economics and business are concerned with the production, distribution and exchange of goods and services in order to meet the needs and wants of customers. Needs and wants are not the same thing. All people have certain needs such as water, food, clothing and shelter. The rich family in Britain needs these just as much as does the poor one in Brazil. Economics and business are about meeting these needs. But human beings tend to want without limit for the sake of enjoyment, once their needs have been satisfied.

Needs	Wants	Difference
Bread	Television	Bread for survival
Clothing	Compact discs	CDs for pleasure
Shelter	Concert tickets	Shelter for survival

Because goods and services have to be made before they can be distributed or exchanged, the part of economics and business theory concerned with production is often referred to as the **creation of wealth**. Thus, the producers of consumer goods (cars, washing machines, dish-washers) and capital goods (lorries, power stations, factories) as well as the money-makers (equity dealers, insurance brokers, commodity dealers) are referred to as **creators of wealth.**

Activity

List four **needs** of a Third World family and compare them with four **wants** of your own family.

3 Scarce resources and choice

Land, labour, capital and enterprise, usually called 'the factors of production', are scarce resources, and choices must be made about alternative uses of them. Sometimes choices are between competing purposes which are good – whether to increase the output of sports shoes or tracksuits; other choices are between conflicting ends – like producing CFC cleaners or 'green' ones. Choosing between goods and services involves cost, and the real cost of choosing one benefit rather than another is called 'opportunity cost', the opportunity you pass by in order to acquire something else. In situations of choice and conflict, personal responsibility enters the decision-making process in an attempt to balance out personal good, the good of others and the good of society.

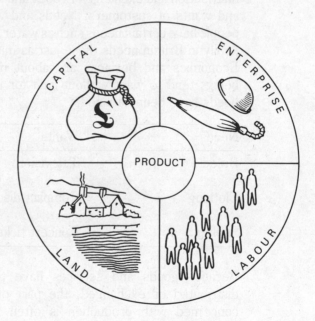

Figure 5
(*From Floyd, D.,*
Business Studies,
Charles Letts and Co.,
London, 1989, p. 1)

Examples of choice and conflict

- Does the Local Planning Committee give permission to build hospitals or leisure centres?
- Do Western governments invest in nuclear arms or in Third World irrigation schemes?
- Do we exhaust supplies of coal and gas or preserve some for future generations?

Activity

List some choices and conflicts and explain the grounds for making selections:

Choices and conflicts	Reasons for selection

4 Scale of values

When trying to find answers to difficult choices and conflicts like those listed above, the immediate inclination is to use your own opinion. The trouble is that there are as many opinions as there are people considering the problem. Economic theory, as a description of business, offers knowledge on what the situation **is** and about possibilities and probabilities for production and distribution. But if we are to decide what **ought** to be done, then we have to use values and principles. This is where ethics comes in. Economics is about facts; it attempts to prove the statements it makes. Business is about quantities, calculation, efficiency. Ethics does not provide answers on its own, but it does offer guidance on what ought to be done in the light of principles and with due consideration of the facts set out by business and economics. Thus, economists and business people, in order to cut down costs and improve efficiency, may pay off workers who are thought to be unnecessary. This is called 'dealing with overmanning'. But ethics, the study of fairness and unfairness, may argue an opposite case on the grounds, say, that certain groups of vulnerable people in security will be particularly badly hit by being unemployed. There is a scale of values in which persons are more important than things, and the needs of the institution are not always more important than those of people.

Keywords

Is/Ought
Fact/Value
Description/Prescription

Activity

Some of these statements are the concern of economists and others of ethicians. Can you sort them out?

1. The Community Charge will bring in more revenue than the old rates system.
2. The Community Charge should be abolished because it takes no account of the ability to pay.
3. A wealth tax would narrow the gap between rich and poor in Britain.
4. Wealth ought to be divided more equally.
5. Mergers increase efficiency.
6. We should conserve scarce resources today for the benefit of future generations.

5 Definitions

Economics   is the study of the allocation of scarce resources among competing claims. This always involves choices and sometimes conflicts.

Business   is the organisation by an entrepreneur of resources for the creation and distribution of wealth.

Business ethics   is the study of the principles and values which guide us in making responsible choices in relation to the possibilities set out by economics and business. It can make *general* statements which are readily accepted by the business community, such as: 'safety standards in air and sea travel are important'; and it can make *particular* statements which people will have to debate and make decisions about, such as: 'safety standards in travel must be improved regardless of cost'.

Dilemma

Read the following case study. Select the solution you think best, and give your reasons for your selection.

Because of the speed with which foam-filled furniture burns and because of the volume of toxic fumes it gives off, all furniture must be made (as from 1 March 1989) from Combustion Modified Foam, and (as from 1 March 1990) must be resistant to a match flame or have a fire-retardant lining.

The management of our (imaginary) company is faced with a dilemma. Ought it to:

(a) Take a loss for management and shareholders and burn all foam-filled furniture next Guy Fawkes night?
(b) Before the set date, sell it to second-hand furniture dealers, who are allowed to sell foam-filled furniture as long as it has passed the less stringent smouldering cigarette test (1983)?
(c) Export it to the Third World at lower prices?

Unit 3 Markets, Freedom and Responsibility

1 Economic systems

There are three types of economic system: *free market* (capitalist); *planned economy* (socialist, centralised, collectivist); and the *mixed economy*. These systems are distinguished from each other by their attitudes to private property, by the degree of acceptance of government intervention in economic activity, and by the role of enterprise and of the individual. Until the autumn of 1989, Europe was divided into two main blocs: the Western and the Eastern. From the point of view of their economic systems, they could be described, roughly, as capitalist and socialist. The West (Britain, France and West Germany etc.) gave more scope to free market forces, while the East (USSR and its satellites) operated a planned economy.

The revolutions in the Eastern bloc have brought changes. Free market forces are now being allowed to organise the allocation of resources. Hungary permitted a stock exchange to be set up in Budapest; and in April 1990, the government of the USSR considered a proposal to do the same.

Figure 6

Activity

Eastern European nations are trying to develop a free market economy. Collect cuttings from newspapers and describe some practical consequences for government and people.

14

The free market system

In theory, this system relies on producers and consumers making decisions about what, how and when to produce and at what prices. Consumer choice governs production, distribution and exchange.

Advantages:

Freedom of choice. People can spend their money as they choose, and in this way they let suppliers know what is being demanded; they can establish their own firms and choose their work.

Efficiency. The free market responds quickly to people's wants. Resources are switched to profitable lines. It encourages the development of new and better technology to produce goods and services. It is dynamic.

Competition. This leads to a wide variety of goods and services being produced to meet consumers' demands.

Incentive. People are encouraged to work in order to take advantage of opportunities, and because they can acquire property and wealth.

Disadvantages:

Profit motive. In a free market system, the profit motive is of first importance to producers, owners, shareholders and management, with the result that they have tended to ignore social costs, such as pollution, though there are signs that business is changing in this regard.

Unequal distribution of wealth. Because power tends to accompany wealth, great disparities between rich and poor can characterise capitalist economies. There can be resistance to fair distribution, though this is not unique to free market economies, being a feature also of planned and of Third World developing economies.

Unemployment and low wages. It is difficult to obtain a free market for labour. In conditions of high unemployment and with an abundance of unskilled labour, the employer has an advantage in this particular labour market. Not so, however, in the demand for skilled labour, which is scarce at present and can command high wages. Because capital is more mobile

Figure 7

than labour, investment plans can be switched if workers show disagreement, as happened recently when Ford Motors changed their plans to invest in Wales and switched to West Germany. Where the above reasons hold good, people offering labour services tend to be at a disadvantage against those who buy their services.

The planned system

In a planned economy, government or public sector make decisions about what to produce, for whom and at what prices. Planners allocate scarce resources.

Advantages:
Use of human resources. Central planning provides high employment and job security.
Large-scale production. Made possible through economies of scale.
Public services (like domestic power) and *basic services* (like health provision) can be provided efficiently.

Disadvantages:
Hidden unemployment: High unemployment is often at the cost of overmanning. It is really hidden unemployment, as can be seen in East German industry, now that it is opened to competition and new ideas of efficiency in a united Germany. The labour-intensive style of planned economies also tends to inhibit technological progress.
Lack of choice.
Little incentive.
Centralised control leads to inefficient bureaucracy.

The mixed economy

In real life there are neither fully free nor fully planned economies. The standard in the West is the mixed economy, which combines freedom of choice with a certain amount of Government planning. In one sense it offers 'the best of both worlds'; but it retains some of the disadvantages of each.

Activity

Make lists of the advantages and the disadvantages of each type of economic system. Describe how the supposed advantages are really what the different systems make them appear to be, and describe them in ethical terms.

Advantages	Disadvantages

Description and ethical comment:

2 Ethical aspects

People are both *acquisitive* and *unselfish*. Note, we do not say selfish and unselfish: selfishness is a fault; acquisitiveness is not.

If an economy is to work, appeal must be made to both instincts. To acquisitiveness, so that people may maximise their outputs; and to unselfishness, so that goods produced may be widely distributed. Attention to the first promotes the creation of wealth; the second secures a just distribution.

But justice is not secured automatically by the operation of impersonal market forces. Freedom of choice and freedom of judgement are basic to the operation of a multiple initiative and enterprise economy (as Eastern European countries have come to learn); but just distribution can only be achieved through the combination of freedom and responsibility. A free market is not to be confused with an uncontrolled market. Market supervision is necessary to market freedom. Freedom is not automatically achieved in a free market economy, neither is equality in a planned one.

Activity

Explain how the following ethical ideas must influence the operations of the three economic systems:

Freedom   *Equality*   *Responsibility*

3　The enterprise culture

The Conservative Government came to power in Britain in 1979 with a programme of liberalisation. Its aim was to deregulate markets and to free the economy. This approach was a reversal of previous thinking which held that market forces must be controlled on moral grounds, since, if left to themselves, they can lead to poverty for many people. The Welfare State, fostering justice and equality of treatment, had been viewed as having a serious *ethical* or *moral* purpose.

The Conservative Government, or the New Right thinking behind it, viewed markets as natural phenomena driven by impersonal forces. The Government's strategy was to pull back the controlling powers in order to allow business to get on with its tasks. This has certainly fostered enterprise, so much so, that Britain is now talked about as influenced by 'an enterprise culture'.

Others argue that markets are not like natural forces: they are the sum total of our own decisions and our own behaviour. We are *responsible* for our own behaviour; it must be ruled by some code of conduct; and the interdependence on which the social system depends will not continue to operate effectively if ability and greed combine to the advantage of the few at the expense of the many.

Dilemma: Fair shares

There are huge disparities in the distribution of wealth in the United Kingdom. The ownership of housing, stocks and shares, property, building society and bank deposits is widely unequal.

The richest	1%	of the population owns	20% of all wealth
The richest	10%	of the population owns	54% of all wealth
The richest	50%	of the population owns	93% of all wealth
The poorest	50%	of the population owns	7% of all wealth

The Government, however, points to two features of economic improvement in the 1980s: the 'ripple effect' (whereby improvement in the South East of England spreads to other regions, as it has done to the Midlands and to Wales, and, it is hoped, eventually further north); and the 'trickle-down effect' (whereby the economic improvement for the top people trickles down to the poorer members of society). Everyone's position improves, though some improve more, and more quickly than others.

A recent Fabian Society report (*Income and Wealth in the 1980s*, 16 July 1990) has cast doubts on the trickle-down effect. It claims that in real terms the top 10% has improved its position by 43%, while the bottom 40% is worse off by up to 8%. Recent Government statistics give some support to this claim.

Consider the inequalities in the distribution of wealth and answer the following questions:

1. Is this situation fair?
2. How can inequalities be reduced?
3. Can the taxation systems help?
4. Is it better to rely on the ripple and trickle-down effects?
5. Can you suggest any other ways?

Unit 4 Does a Business have a Conscience?

1 Individual and social responsibility

Helena Jones is manager of Marketing Research in the fictitious O.K. Biscuit Company Limited. Recently, her department has slacked off and performance has declined. A review of the department's work reveals that Helena's daughter has been in hospital; and, as a single-parent, this has put the mother under extra stress. She cannot afford to be without full-time work, and she has to fit in as many visits to the hospital as she can. As a consequence of her personal worry, she has allowed her responsibilities to her department to slip.

In this situation there are conflicting ethical claims on Ms Jones. She has individual ethical and moral responsibilities to support and visit her sick daughter. By virtue of her contract of employment, she has further individual responsibilities of managerial competence and performance to her firm. These individual responsibilities have a social aspect, since Helena Jones is part of a business institution to whose survival, efficiency and profitability she contributes.

Activity

Helena Jones has a number of options. She could:

1. Go sick and get a doctor's certificate
2. Resign
3. Explain the situation and ask to take some holiday leave
4. Ask for a transfer to part-time work.

Which option would you take? Give your reasons.

2 The company's social responsibility

Up to this point we have been looking at the situation from the point of view and conscience of Helena Jones. But what about the responsibilities and conscience of the company?

To talk about '*a company's social responsibilities*' is an impersonal form of description, and in ethics it is preferable to make moral decisions refer, where possible, to persons. In talking about a company's moral responsibilities, we are often referring to the duties of directors, who have numerous responsibilities:

(a) to shareholders;
(b) to managers;
(c) to employees;
(d) to suppliers and clients;
(e) to their families and the wider community.

As with employees, conflicts arise for directors in trying to satisfy their range of responsibilities. They are responsible for company policy and for being faithful to the ethos or outlook of the company. Take the case of a publisher of religious books. Clearly, a publishing firm of this kind must have a higher vision than the publisher of a tabloid newspaper, and the directors must be concerned to get the 'message' over. On the other hand, they have responsibilities to their shareholders and to their workers, and must not become so overwhelmed by the message that profits fall so much that the company is put at risk.

The prime imperative of the company is that it should be efficient *and* responsible. Business ethics, however, must address the question of the efficient use of resources and of an effective sales policy and practice. For years, your local light engineering firm has bought certain parts from a small family firm. But the engineering business is expanding to keep up with increased demand, and not only can the family firm not meet targets, but a larger firm has come into the market and offers to supply the parts at 20% less than you have been paying. The need for efficiency is in tension with existing responsibilities to the old family firm you have been dealing with.

The problems being described here cannot be solved by the application of any simple rules. Many factors have to be kept in mind and the ethics of directors' responsibilities must include experience and wisdom which keeps in balance responsibilities to the five groups mentioned above. We might say that there is a general principle that all directors have a duty to preserve the 'lean and hungry' approach to business, but not at the price of disregarding all other considerations.

Activity

In the case of Helena Jones, the company's estimate is that she is not fulfilling her contract: she is costing the company money; she is contributing to the decline in the performance of her department. They can either sack her, or look for some other solution. Provide your own solution to the problem. Use the following questions as a checklist of whether you have made an ethical decision:

1. Have you defined the problem accurately?

2. How would you define the problem if you were looking at it,
   (a) from Helena's point of view?
   (b) from the Managing Director's point of view?

3. To whom do you owe your loyalty as a person and as a member of the company?

4. What is your intention in making this decision?

5. How does your intention relate to the probable results?

6. Whom could your decision hurt?

7. Will your decision stand the test of time, or is it a short-term remedy?

8. Under what circumstances would you allow exceptions to your present decision?

3 Organisation, goals, and making companies responsible

Financial success, however, is not the only measure of company performance; and business ethics must take account of other company values and practices. In establishing the aims and objectives, directors must remember that the company exists to serve people, and that profit is a means to an end. Employees must not be treated just as means to profit.

The scientific approach to courses of business studies and commerce, and the pressure of business life all work together to emphasise organisational, efficiency and other impersonal aspects of the company, so that the individual may be seen only as a number.

Here is a typical organisation chart of a company:

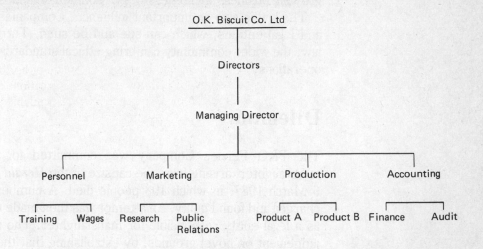

Because it is a hierarchical system with lines of command similar to army structure, the organisation chart and its goals, coupled with the imperative of financial success, can blind directors to the reality that the company is composed of people involved in a cooperative exercise. One way around this is for the company to adopt an open-management style – popular in Germany – which involves managers and other employees in the company's aims and objectives, and which are set out in a mutually agreed company plan. This gets away from the idea that directors have responsibility only to the *shareholders*. Everybody who is affected by the business is a *stakeholder:* shareholders obviously are, but so also are employees, former employees to whom pensions are being paid, suppliers, customers and the community at large. The Managing Director's job is to state, as fairly as possible, the company's objectives in respect of each of the five sets of stakeholders mentioned in section 2 above.

Making companies responsible

Strictly speaking, companies are not persons; and only persons can be exactly described as having ethical and moral duties. In certain respects, however, ideas and functions which are literally applied to persons can also be applied to institutions made up of persons. Goals, values and strategies are applied to organisations; and in the same way we may talk of a 'company conscience'. The effective voice of this conscience lies with the leadership (directors and managers), who play the key-role as a bridge between individual and organisational values.

A company conscience, however, can be influenced by consumer pressure and public opinion. A report by Peat Marwick Consultants (June

1990) stated that 'green' pressure groups had been a main force behind growing business awareness of environmental issues.

The law is also an important influence. Companies are 'moral persons' and legal entities, which can sue and be sued. Through recourse to the law, the wider community can bring ethical standards to bear on company operations.

Dilemma

The P&O Ferries Company was committed for trial on charges of manslaughter, arising from the capsize of the *Herald of Free Enterprise* on 6 March 1987, in which 193 people died. A number of individuals were charged and found guilty. An attempt was then made to make the company as a legal entity responsible for manslaughter. The prosecution sought a judgement on novel grounds: by establishing that the acts of a number of individuals, not just those of the controlling officers, amount to gross responsible for the sum total of individual negligent acts. However, the prosecution failed.

Consider and decide:

1. Whether the above company ought to have been held responsible for a capsize that occurred to a ferry leaving harbour with its bow doors open.
2. Whether any company can be held corporately responsible for the negligences of a number of its individual employees; or are only the owners responsible?

Give your reasons.

Unit 5 | Managers and Leadership

1 Managers' values and attitudes

Businessmen are often their own worst enemy. We read in the newspaper reports that the prosecution in the alleged Guinness scandal trial in the Crown Court said that Mr Saunders was so anxious to win the bid he was making that he made secret and illegal agreements to boost Guinness shares, neither caring for the public who might be cheated nor the shareholders whose funds would be squandered. When we read this we shrug our shoulders and say, 'What do you expect from businessmen?' In the same way, we consider the thousands of people who entrusted their money to Barlow Clowes to secure good investments for their old age, as foolish to have done so.

Leadership is not confined to the people at the top of the company, but they do have special responsibilities for maintaining values and attitudes which set the moral tone. One important part of business ethics is assisting the leaders, especially managers, to reflect on the problems and challenges facing them as they try to cope with difficult choices in their business.

The problems can come from above. Suppose you are a manager of a first-class hotel. One of your board directors visits regularly, and after each visit a bottle of whisky goes missing. You know where it has gone; and so does your bar manager (and through him, many of the waiters know as well). You do not want to offend the director; but to ignore the matter means setting a bad example and allowing moral standards to slide. That is trouble from someone at the top; but trouble can come from below as well. There is, for example the problem of 'shrinkage', which occurs when workers, say, in a store take things without paying for them. It is a sort of internal shoplifting. Managers should never turn a blind eye to these practices. If they do, you get a 'downward spiral of ethics in business'. Management has a key role to play in setting high standards of conduct which will lead to an upwards spiral in business ethics.

Activities

A Swedish firm making household appliances recently took over a small British company in the same field. The new directors explained that good housekeeping, cleanliness and tidiness, were viewed in Sweden as having a good effect on efficiency and production. Management were asked to give a lead. They responded by improving the lighting in the workshops; by installing ways of keeping the floors dry in the production sheds; by reorganising meal times, catering and short work breaks; by seeing to regular sweeping and cleanliness; by making new transport arrangements for workers from the local housing estate. These rather obvious improvements had a knock-on effect on efficiency and on industrial and human relationships in the business.

1

List some other ways in which management could give a lead.

2

List some ethical considerations in this situation.

2 Varying values

Business ethics must find ways of getting managers to assess whether or not they are accepting the duties and challenges to set the moral tone. One way of doing this is to examine the questions they ask themselves when making business decisions. One study of managerial values classified managers according to three key questions:

1. Will it work?
2. Is it right?
3. Is it pleasant?

Results from five different countries are shown below, indicating the priority that managers give to three considerations:

	USA	Japan	Korea	Australia	India
Will it work? (Pragmatic approach)	57.3%	67.4%	53.1%	40.2%	52.9%
Is it right? (Ethical approach)	30.3%	9.9%	9.0%	40.2%	44.1%
Is it pleasant? (Emotive approach)	1.2%	7.0%	8.5%	5.4%	2.2%
Mixed	11.2%	15.8%	29.4%	14.2%	19.6%
No. of managers	997	374	211	351	623

From: Davis, K. and Frederick, W., *Business and Society*, 5th edn, McGraw-Hill, New York, 1984, p. 55.

Analysis of findings

The most striking contrast in the table is between the very low score registered by Japan and Korea and the much higher score of USA, Australia and India on the ethical approach. In the case of India, ethical considerations were put higher (44.1%) than those of efficiency (34.0%). USA, Australia and India (whose management has been greatly influenced by British ideas) do have a set of ethical values in business which are not part of the Japanese and Korean approach. But this does not mean that the latter have no business ethics. What the high score on the pragmatic approach seems to indicate is that effectiveness is seen by them as an ethical value, in the same way that work became a characteristic value of the Protestant ethic in the West. All the countries score high on efficiency, with USA and Japan registering particularly high scores: the lesson that this drives home is that ethics in business must respect the bottom line, which is that profit is necessary and it cannot be achieved without pragmatic considerations.

The overreaching commitment of Japanese management is to efficiency and productivity, and this has encouraged a style which fosters employee involvement, which is looked on as a long-term relationship. Employees are rarely dismissed. Management has a sense of responsibility for welfare and development. Here is a strand of thinking which indicates that it is good when there is no confrontation between business and ethics, but that business efficiently conducted produces good human consequences, which the Japanese may not think of as 'ethical', even though that is the way we would describe them.

Australia provides an interesting equal weight to pragmatic and ethical approaches (40.2%). This has been attributed to the high religious outlook of public and commercial life, as a consequence of ethnic origins.

Activities

1

Write a short comment on the table which has just been discussed, drawing out ethical aspects of the findings.

2

In Nissan's car plant in Sunderland, the style of production and of management–employee relationships is more cooperative than hierarchical. Technology has been adapted from a line system (in which workers stick strictly to their specialised task) and, instead, workers are involved in many parts of the car assembly. In this way they see the product as much more their own work. Assembly and quality is controlled in circular fashion (hence the term 'quality circles' as a description of this method of working). Participation in the enterprise, cooperation in the setting of medium-term objectives and flexible working hours all contribute to an ethos of cooperation. This dimension of ownership extends also to social aspects of the firm, since managers and all employees share all facilities and dining room services.

(a) Even if, in a sense, Nissan uses people as a means to an end of improving productivity, can it not be said, nevertheless, that their approach is ethical?

(b) Japanese management achieves success partly by getting its medium-term objectives clear. Is it not both sound business and good ethics to make sure, in Japanese style, that middle-managers have a clear idea of medium-term objectives and that these are made known to the other workers?

(c) Is there a sense in which sound business ethics requires all employees to be managers?

Listing managers' values

Further light was shed on managers' values in a 1982 survey of 1,400 managers, who ranked important managerial values as follows:

Managers' list		Your list
1. Responsible	(88%)	
2. Honest	(88%)	
3. Capable	(67%)	
4. Imaginative	(55%)	
5. Logical	(49%)	
6. Ambitious	(37%)	

Write your own list of the six most important values for managers, putting them in order of importance. State your reasons for including them, and explain why you put them in the order you did.

3 Why good managers make unethical decisions

When asked to rank factors which might influence them to make unethical decisions, readers of the *Harvard Business Review* listed "behaviour of superiors in the company" as number 1.

Reasons for being unethical

	1982 survey	1977 survey	Your list
Behaviour of one's superiors	1	1	?
Behaviour of one's equals	2	4	?
Industry's ethical climate	3	3	?
Society's moral climate	4	5	?
Company's policy or lack of one	5	2	?
Personal financial need	6	6	?

Activity

List, in order of importance, the factors which might influence you to make unethical decisions.

Dilemma

In the 1970s, Firestone marketed its Radial 500 tyre, which had a higher-than-average accident rate. Although under strong pressure from Government, the company refused to withdraw it, because the industry world-wide was undergoing a competitive shakeout due to overcapacity and falling sales. Taking Radial 500 off the market would have meant severe damage to Firestone's position (Natale, S. *Ethics and Decision Making*, Institute for Business and Management Ethics, Iona College, New York, 1989, p. 16).

1. Would you have argued for loyalty to the company and shareholders, and so have kept the tyre on the market?

2. Would you have kept the tyre on sale in order to protect employees' jobs?

3. Would you have put the safety of customers and the community first?

Figure 8

4 A company's code of ethics

The values and attitudes of management can be set out in a Code of Ethics. The Managing Director must be the driving force behind it.

The Body Shop has a Code of Ethics available to all. It is set out in a leaflet entitled *What is the Body Shop?* Here is a summary:

- We use vegetable rather than animal ingredients.
- We do not test on animals.
- We are environmental conscious, using recycled paper and producing biodegradable goods.

- We use naturally-based ingredients as far as possible.
- We keep packaging to a minimum.
- We source many of our products in the Third World.
- We have established a relationship to help the Boys' Town Trust in South India.
- Our products reflect our philosophy.

The Body Shop philosophy is that its business is a *"partnership of profits with principles."* The ethical tone of the company is clearly established by the management, who "want to give something back to society."

Activities

1

List some ways in which a company could give back something beneficial to society.

2

Make another list of harmful things which companies give back to society.

---

5 ## ABOUT BRITISH TELECOM

section

CODE OF PRACTICE FOR CONSUMERS

Figure 9

British Telecom's Telephone Services

The British Telecommunications network

8 The telephone services provided by British Telecom as a network operator under its

that your entry is accurate and up-to-date each time the Phone Book is reprinted, but occasionally accidental errors will occur.

15 If your entry is omitted from the Phone Book, or is seriously wrong, you should inform your local British Telecom office as soon as possible. We cannot do a special reprint of the Phone Book but we will try to help you by suggesting one or more of a wide variety of measures. These may include supplying printed cards (which can be returned to British Telecom for free despatch) to send to friends or paying for a notice in the

it is presented, contact your local British Telecom office for advice on methods of payment. This may avoid your telephone service being disconnected and remove the need for further recovery action.

25 In certain circumstances, where the use of a telephone is essential, it is suggested you contact the Social Services Department of your local authority who may be able to assist you.

RECONNECTION OF SERVICE
26 There is normally a fee for reconnecting

Unit 6 Ethics and the Consumer

1 Competition and advertising

In the real world it is unlikely that we will find the situation of perfect competition, where there are many small firms competing for the best use of resources in the sale of one product. In this situation, demand and supply are in balance at the price offered in the market; profit is 'normal', and exploitation is not possible.

What is more likely is the situtaion where a few large companies (oligopoly) control, or one large company (monopoly) controls, the supply of a commodity to the market. The terms are relative. In British law, for example, a monopoly is defined as any firm or group of firms supplying 25% or more of a market. In these markets, particularly in monopolies, there is restricted competition, and profits can be abnormally high. The company or companies are price-makers rather than price-takers, so that barriers are erected to free entry into the market.

Dentists, by specialised knowledge and skills, have a certain monopoly position in society. Under National Health Service arrangements their fee structure allows them

£5 for an extraction
£15 for a filling
£50 for crowning a tooth

The scale is structured in favour of preventative dentistry; which is good. But if dentists crown teeth in order to take a higher fee, when a simpler job would do (as some dentists in interview admitted) then they would be acting unethically.

In conditions of monopoly or ologopoly, pressure to make potential customers buy products is achieved through advertising or other forms of sales pressures, such as postal sales, promises of loans and credit facilities.

Advertising is big business (see Figure 10). In Britain, £5,000 million is spent annually on advertising.

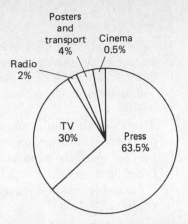

Activities

1

Advertising: fair or unfair?
Watch a sample of 5 television adverts; listen to 5 radio adverts; collect 5 printed or newspaper adverts. Keeping in mind the basic ethical ideas from Unit 1 (**honesty; trust; fairness; respect for persons**), make up your mind whether each advert:

(a) gives truthful information;
(b) is acting as 'a hidden persuader';
(c) makes meaningless statements;
(d) suggests that buying the product will improve quality of life;
(e) is sexist or racist.

List the 15 products in your selection of adverts and tick them off on a check list, and see if there is any pattern to advertising which might allow you to make general ethical statements about it.

Product advertised	Informative	Persuasive	Meaningless	Quality of life	Sexist	Racist
1						
2						
3						
4						
5						
6						
7						
8						
9						
10						
11						
12						
13						
14						
15						

> **2**
>
> *Information rather than advertising*
> Instead of advertising, Ecover (which is an environment-friendly detergent) and the Body Shop offer open information on their products and business practices, and allow the customers to make up their own minds.
> They claim that this is non-exploitative, in the sense that no external pressure is put on prospective buyers to choose a particular product, but they are given the information and allowed to make up their own minds. Freedom is preferred to pressure.
> Write a short essay comparing these two styles of recommending one's products.

2 Sales pressure, the customer and the law

In Britain there are laws and strict rules to control the sale of many products, to protect trading standards, to provide consumer protection and to regulate forms of advertising.

(a) *Monopolies and Mergers Commission*

This body exists to investigate and report on monopolies and mergers between firms, in order to see if these firms are acting in the interest of consumers. For example, following a report by the Commission, the Government (July 1990) proposed that the takeover of Portsmouth Citybus by the Stagecoach Bus Company be unwound, on the grounds that the merger has acted against the public interest by wiping out competition. There is concern that the aims of the Bus Industry Deregulation provisions of 1986 are being undermined through excessive concentration of ownership.

(b) *Restrictive Practices Court*

This is a statutory institution which tries to control groups of firms acting together to create a monopoly and to keep competition out of the industry.

(c) *Office of Fair Trading*

Created by the Fair Trading Act of 1976, this is a Government agency which keeps a watch on the conduct of trade and protects the consumer against unfair practices. The Director General of Fair Trading has received important new powers under the Control of Misleading Advertising Regulations (1988). His powers cover adverts in:

- newspapers and magazines
- outdoor locations, such as buses, taxis and posters
- cinema commercials
- brochures, leaflets, display material, circulars and direct mail.

(d) *Advertising Standards Authority*

This is a self-regulatory body established in 1962 by the advertising industry to protect the interests of consumers. It oversees the British Code of Sales Promotion Practice and the British Code of Advertising Practice which require that the content of all advertisements and sales promotion in non-broadcast material is legal, decent, honest and truthful, and prepared with a sense of responsibility to the consumer and to society. Advertisers are required to conform not only to the rules contained in the Codes, but also to their *spirit*.

In addition to investigating and publishing complaints from members of the public, the ASA has a duty to monitor advertisements in all national, regional and specialist publications throughout the UK. If an advert offends either of the Codes, the advertiser is asked to withdraw or amend it as appropriate. It is unusual to find an advertiser refusing to do as he is asked, but if this happens the ASA send out a media warning. Publishers are required not to accept advertisements which are against the Codes, so that, following a media warning, the advertiser will not be able to place his advert.

Although the ASA is a self-regulatory body, the Control of Misleading Advertisements Regulation (1988) gives the Authority statutory back-up. If all ASA's efforts prove fruitless, it can refer an advertiser to the Director-General of Fair Trading in order to prevent him from disseminating misleading advertising. Since the Regulations came into effect in June 1988, the ASA has had to refer only three advertisers to the Office of Fair Trading.

The ASA handles many complaints itself. For example, in July 1990 it received four complaints from members of the public against advertisements for British Rail's Inter-City Service. These adverts claimed that rail travel is more relaxing and less stressful than air travel. The complainants denied this on their own experience. In its defence, BR claimed that it had never said that "passengers never had to run for trains" or that "Inter-City were free from interruption!" But the ASA rejected these arguments and warned BR to take "greater care" when making comparisons.

The ASA also has an industry arm, the Committee of Advertising Practice, which investigates competitive complaints and provides free copy advice to advertisers and agencies on their advertisements prior to publication. This Committee drafts the Codes and various guidelines and implements them on behalf of the ASA. The representatives on this Committee can be found listed on the inside cover of the British Code of Advertising Practice.

The ASA is clearly an important supervisory body of an ethical type, and the significance of its role can be judged from the amount and kind of complaints received by ASA between July 1988 and June 1989:

Number of complaints
Pursued   8,095
Not pursued   3,393

Examples of type
Mail order delay   751
Copy content   643

Top ten product groups reported

1. Computer products   61
2. Cars   48
3. Financial   43
4. Holiday/hotels   37
5. Recruitment   32
6. Travel   29
7. Property/estate agents   27
8. Treatments   26
9. Furniture   20
10. Publishers   17

Activities

1

List examples of the particular complaints which might be made under the above headings. For example, your holiday hotel brochure advertised your hotel as "looking out onto the beach," but when you got there you found it was a bus-ride away.

2

Discuss The Advertising Standards Authority as a model for business ethics in the way it combines control by rules with attention to the spirit of the rules.

3 Sales pressure, the customer and business ethics

The statutory bodies and the Advertising Standards Authority have considerable teeth. If they ban an advertisement, no television station, radio station, newspaper or magazine will accept it. From the point of view of ethics, then, it can be claimed that these bodies do establish a basis for correct values in buying and selling goods and services. But in spite of this effective regulation, further moral obligations do arise between companies and their customers. It is not true that business people can do what they like as long as they keep within the law, or that anything goes as long as you are not caught, or that 'small' wrongs are all right if they do not break the law. If ethics is going to be taken seriously, business people must look at the potential consequences of their actions on customers and ask whether they are prepared to take personal responsibility for such actions.

Real dilemmas may arise when a company is tempted to supply goods which are legal, but may harm customers. The tobacco industry provides an obvious example. The medical evidence that smoking damages health and may cause lung cancer is overwhelming. In a free society, it may be argued, each person should be allowed to make the decision for himself or herself whether to smoke or not. As long as the government warning is put on every packet, that is enough. But tobacco companies need to ask whether they should accept responsibility for promoting a product which is widely believed to damage health and sometimes lead to early death.

Or, take the case of remould tyres. Third World countries need vehicles and spare parts. Remoulds may be sold to them at cheap prices. But they are less safe; and given the rough land conditions and the difficulty of imposing safe driving regulations, the risks of accident are high. It is not against the law to sell such tyres, but are there not ethical requirements going beyond the law?

Dilemma

A computer firm is confident that it is on the verge of producing an attractive new Desktop Publishing package. It is also having cash flow problems at the moment. Should it:

(a) Advertise the product in advance of completion and begin to take orders in advance?
(b) Advertise on completion but ahead of exhaustive testing?
(c) Deal in other ways with cash flow problems and not put its potential customers at any risk?

Activities

1

Go to your local public reference library and ask for information on the Advertising Standards Authority.

2

Here are seven Golden Rules to follow before you buy anything by post:

(a) Check that the newspaper, magazine or catalogue is up-to-date.

(b) If you buy through a newspaper or magazine advert, check whether you are covered by a protection scheme. If you are not, and pay in advance, you could lose your money if the business fails.

(c) If you have to send money, never send cash by post.

(d) When you write (and when you return goods) always include your name and address.

(e) Always keep a copy of your order and the date it was sent.

(f) Keep a copy of the advert or the name and address of the advertiser and all details of the advert.

(g) If you have a complaint, make sure you give full details of your advert and of your order.

Use these rules as the basis of a class discussion of 'ethics in buying and selling'.

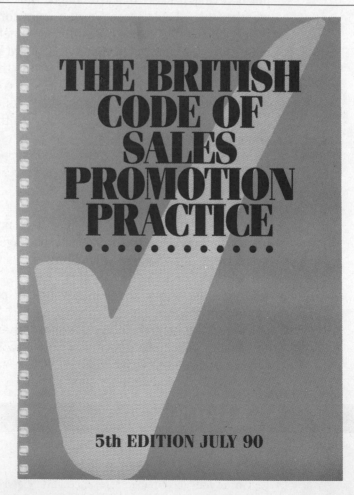

Figure 11

Unit 7 Employers and Employees

1 An ethic of partnership

A simple picture is sometimes presented of the relationship of employer and employee. When an employee joins a company, he or she agrees wages and terms and conditions of employment, which must be set down in a written contract of employment not later than thirteen weeks after the verbal agreement. (The contract does not apply, of course, in the case of part-time workers, as we have seen in Unit 1). The employee is seen as having a duty to serve the company to the best of his or her ability, in return for which he or she receives a weekly wage packet or monthly salary.

This picture does not do justice to the realities. The model on which it is based is a paternalistic one in which the employee's task is clear. The truth is that life at work is as full of tales of the unexpected as tales of mystery. As the employee gains experience 'on the job', especially in the flexible and partnership arrangements which are beginning to take hold in British industry, early expectations are changed. The employee may gain the advantage of a training scheme, which might end up to the disadvantage of the company, as in the case of the young worker in an import–export firm, who was sent to Spain for 3 months to develop his language skills, and then left the firm for a better job. Was this a right, ethical, thing to do?

Furthermore, company policy and management change over a period (to say nothing of changes in the law) and new situations arise. When the tacheograph was introduced into lorry cabs a few years ago, restricting the hours that drivers might do in a day, this involved rearranging schedules and altering shift work and bonus earnings. There can be changes, too, in the conditions of markets which affect company policy and practice. In the recent salmonella scare concerning eggs, personnel in egg marketing suddenly found themselves on part-time work or made redundant. In this changing and dynamic situation, employers and employees need to be able to respond to each other. There must be a recognition that capital needs labour just as labour needs capital. The appropriate model for employer–employee relationships is one of partnership, from which would flow a recognition of the need to be responsive to rights, duties and problems.

Example

You are a long-distance van driver, working for a small firm and carrying antiques between London and the Continent of Europe. The limit for the weight load of the van is 20 tons, but because the firm is finding it difficult to survive in competition with a number of large operators, you are asked by the management to carry 25 tons. To do so is to break the law, and if you are stopped for a spot check you may lose your licence. But if you do not agree to take the extra load, you may lose your job.

1. Would you obey the management?
2. Would you obey the law?
3. Would you try to resolve the matter in discussion with management before taking to the road?
4. Would you seek advice from your trade union?

Obedience to conscience

The problem is not always a matter of law so much as a matter of conscience. You may, for example, be working in a small garage which sells second-hand cars. The boss may ask you to turn back the mileage reading in order to raise the selling price of the car; or he may get you to patch up rust corrosion in order to conceal serious faults.

Activity

Read these case studies, where conscience and managerial practice come into conflict, and answer the key questions set out below:

Case 1   A kitchen assistant, working in a firm selling take-away pizzas, thinks that customer health is being put at risk by unhygienic practices. The management is unconcerned. Should the assistant go to the Local Health Department?

Case 2   A man works for a scaffolding firm which takes on numerous small jobs. The scaffolding is below standard and is not being erected with the utmost safety precautions. Management's attitude is that 'it is not up long enough for anyone to take notice'. But the workman complains to the Local Council Building Control department.

Case 3   A woman buys herself into a partnership in a firm of estate agents. She soon realizes that office managers pretend to receive higher offers, in order to push up the prices. Since she is now benefiting financially, she does nothing.

Checklist questions

(a) Will anyone, not aware of what is happening and of the risk involved, be hurt?

(b) Will the employee put his or her job at risk by refusing to comply with orders?

(c) Has the line of action being commended become the norm for the industry?

(d) Will the ethical stand being recommended make any difference to the situation?

2 Duties of employers

Partnership is not a passive relationship, but includes, rather, an active ethical or moral responsibility for the welfare of employees. At the most basic level, this means that management must be vigilant about the safety and health of employees. Recently, the Director General of the Health and Safety Commission (set up under the Health and Safety at Work Act, 1974) warned employers:

"Our business is to pin the responsibility where it belongs – on the directors and managements of enterprises."

This indicates that authorities and industry do care about ethical matters, and there has been a great improvement in health and safety vigilance, though there are exceptions. A report in the *Financial Times*, 13 July 1990, refers to the case of the Transmanche Link Channel Tunnel Construction Company. An enquiry by the Health and Safety Executive's Accident Prevention Advisory Unit into the death of six building workers on the UK side as compared with two on the French side, found weak and uncoordinated safety management on the project. Pointing to the risk of 'catastrophic loss of life', the Executive warned contractors to improve safety controls. A seventh man has since died.

Activities

1

Study the graphs in Figure 12 (on page 42).
In which year were there most fatalities?
In this year, compare the number of employees who died with the number of self-employed. What lessons might be learned?

2

The Health and Safety Executive's Factory Inspectorate is understaffed at present, with four years' overdue inspections pending. Discuss ethical aspects of this backlog.

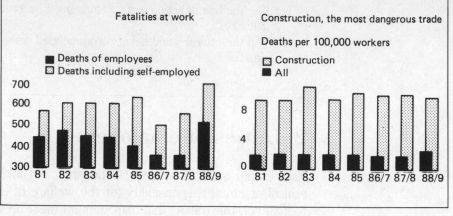

Figure 12
(*From* Sunday
Observer, *6 May
1990*)

3 Duties of employees

Partnership also affects the duties of employees to the company; and this is one area in which unethical or wrong practices are often taken for granted. In office work, it is easy to slip into a habit of taking stationery (pens, typewriter ribbons); teachers and university staff make free use of photocopying facilities; sales representatives draw petrol on a company account, and then use it for private purposes.

Question: If these practices are sanctioned, in the sense that employers 'turn a blind eye' to them, are they morally acceptable?

4 European social charter

With only one dissenting voice – that of Mrs Thatcher – the Social Charter was adopted at the Strasbourg summit on 8 December 1989. The force of the 'social charter' can be gathered from its full name, the *Community Charter of the Fundamental Social Rights of Workers*, and it sets out an ethical basis for employees under 12 headings:

1. the free movement of workers within the Economic Community;
2. 'fair' remuneration for employment;
3. the improvement and approximation of conditions of employment;
4. social security;
5. freedom of association and collective bargaining;
6. vocational training;
7. equal treatment for men and women;
8. information, consultation and participation arrangements;
9. health and safety at the workplace;
10. young people;
11. retired people;
12. disabled people.

5 Ethics of 'stakeholding'

Among the provisions of the social charter, number 8 refers to how information, consultation and participation arrangements should be shared with all employees. After 1992, European Company Statute will require companies to adopt a model for enabling employees to "participate in the supervision and strategic development" of their companies.

The basic premise of this statute is that every individual working in the company is a 'stakeholder' and should share in rewards and decision-making. This does not mean that rewards should be shared equally or that all decisions can be taken by all employees. Details of sharing need to be worked out, but the principle is stated in the statute.

An important form of sharing in rewards which is becoming a focus of interest in Britain is that of workers' share-ownership. In the form of ESOPs (Employee Share Ownership Plan) and PEPs (Personal Equity Plans) it received recognition in the 1989 Finance Act. ESOPs is a system by which management sets up a trust inside the company, which buys shares and then allows workers to purchase them at 80% of their market value. PEPs are tax-free schemes to encourage wider share-ownership.

These schemes are actively encouraged by the Government; but some companies, because they are uneasy about the requirement in them to reward all workers equally, find them unattractive and prefer similar arrangements which do not fall within the statutory definition. The financial sector is keen to encourage the statutory plans and is funding companies to enable them to buy shares to give to their employees.

The table below demonstrates the growth in this kind of shareownership:

Take-up of shares in all-employee share schemes

	Value of shares in year (£m)	Present value (£m)
1980	50	230
1981	85	323
1982	215	495
1983	248	570
1984	264	502
1985	730	1,146
1986	580	748
1987	740	932
1988	1,000	1,222
1989	1,320	1,320
Total	5,232	7,488

Source: *The Share Centre/Corporate Communication Strategy.*

It may be claimed that this is an ethical development. Business ethics is not a pre-conceived moral scheme imposed on business from outside, even from on high. It is a moral interpretation worked out in the context of business itself. Because the whole aggregate of the millions of little decisions and actions which people take in connection with the firms and work can change organisations, attitudes and commercial interests, and because, in connection with shareholding, these seem to assist human development, it may be claimed that the extension of share-ownership demonstrates business ethics at work.

Activities

1

Look at the financial pages of *The Telegraph, The Times, The Independent, The Guardian* or the *Financial Times* for adverts about ESOPs and PEPs. Who is placing the adverts? What conclusions do you draw?

2

Find out all you can about ESOPs and PEPs. You can write to the Confederation of British Industries for this information.

3

Mrs Jenkins, working part-time for Kingsgate Ltd of Harlow, a company producing women's clothes, was earning 10% less per hour than full-time employees. Most of the part-time workers in the Harlow company were women, and in 1981 this was construed by the European Court of Justice as constituting sexual discrimination. National courts must apply this in the light of their own circumstances. The Court took a similar line in 1986, after Mr Weber challenged the refusal of the Bilka shops in Frankfurt to provide a supplementary pension for their part-time workers.

Give your reasons why women workers are more likely to suffer discrimination of the kind outlined above.

Unit 8 | Business as a Friend of the Universe

1 Social costs and ethical responsibility

A paint company is looking at the possibility of locating a new factory near Greenwich. The company estimates that the annual costs of the new factory will be £8 million, but that annual sales should top £10 million. From the point of view of *private* costs and benefits, the investment is commercially sound.

The local community, however, is worried about the effects of smoke and harmful chemicals on the atmosphere. Initial investigations suggest that these will contribute to acid rain, with damaging results to soil and rivers. Additionally, the Local Health Authority estimates that hospital and health bills will rise. These external costs are computed at £3 million.

The County Council reckons further that smoke damage and erosion of historic buildings will add some £2 million per annum to preservation and cleaning.

There will, however, be some external benefits. Local transport will benefit, as will caterers, shops and restaurants. Local unemployment will be reduced, and other businesses may be attracted to the area. External benefits are calculated at £2 million.

Sound economic decisions will be based on the total cost to society, taking private costs and benefits along with external costs and benefits. In other words, it is *social* costs which should be decisive. Economic decisions, then, should not be based only on grounds of private profitability. They should include consideration of effects on the community and the wider world, and, even, of aspects which are not readily measurable. For example, logging and cattle ranching may make good commercial sense in parts of the Brazilian forests, but not at the expense of the way of life of the native Indian population or, for that matter, of the importance of rain forests.

Activities

1

Which costs does the paint company consider when setting up the factory?

2

Estimate private and external costs and benefits, and give the social costs.

3

Imagine that you are a local representative for the Green Party sent to negotiate with the company and planning authority. Take basic social costs and any other considerations you may consider relevant, and prepare a short paper setting out an ethical case for or against location.

2 Growing ethical awareness

At a local level, and faced with locating *one* factory, it is possible for the management to arrive at some realistic assessment of social costs as a guide to investment decisions. But at an international level, and faced with the almost immeasurable consequences of complex technology and large-scale investment, social costs become inestimable. For these reasons, and sometimes also for commercial advantage, businesses have, in the past, ignored social costs.

In the past decade, however, business has begun to show a growing awareness of the need to consider social costs. In the industrialised world in particular, there has recently been a revolution in recognising the importance of caring for the environment. This is the so-called 'green revolution'. Under intense public and political pressure, companies admit that they must tackle a broad range of pollution problems. New legislation and strict controls will have an impact on the way industry operates and on the type of product it will develop. But it would be naive to think that all decisions which turn out to be ethically good are taken for ethical reasons: they may be taken for commercial reasons. But then we have a case of 'good business is good ethics'. For example, the increasing awareness of the need to care for the environment may be fostered for commercial reasons. It is obvious that there is a ready-made market for expertise and technology to take advantage of the new environmental clean-up. Thus, the United Kingdom output of pollution-control equipment and services is thought to have earned about £3.8 billion in 1988; and the world market is estimated as worth £100 billion.

Here is a list of issues connected with industry and the environment, which have global effects endangering the future of mankind:

1. The greenhouse effect; global warming; ozone layer; tropical rain forests.
2. Fossil fuels, carbon dioxide pollution, nuclear fuels, conservation of energy.
3. The chemical industry, with a global turnover of $1,000 billion per annum, has problems of dangerous gases/liquid emissions, ozone damage, over-use of agro-chemicals and waste disposal.
4. Oil spillage.
5. Pollution of seas, rivers and waterways.
6. Industrial chemicals in food.
7. Car exhaust emission and lead poisoning.

Activities

1

Study the following tables and write a short comment on pollution and industry's growing awareness of its responsibilities.

Further data obtainable from: Association for the Conservation of Energy, London (telephone: 071–935 1495).

Pollution – UK emissions by source, proportions of total (percentages), 1988

SECTOR	Sulphur dioxide	Nitrogen oxides	Carbon monoxide	Carbon dioxide	Black smoke
Domestic	4	3	7	15	42
Commercial/public service	3	2	–	6	1
Power stations	71	32	1	33	5
Refineries	3	1	–	3	–
Agriculture	–	–	–	–	–
Other industry	17	12	6	24	17
Rail transport	–	1	–	–	–
Road transport	1	45	85	18	34
Shipping	–	3	–	1	–
TOTAL	100	100	100	100	100

Source: *Warren Spring Laboratory, Department of Trade & Industry (© Crown Copyright 1990 by permission)*.

Gross annual cost of pollution control by private sector industry, 1988 (1986 prices)

Industry	Gross costs £ million (1986 prices)	Share %
Chemicals	390	25
Food processing	314	20
Fuels processing	34	2
Metal manufacture	279	18
Paper and pulp	222	14
Engineering	126	8
Quarrying and cement	99	6
Other manufacturing	93	6
Total Industry costs	1,557	100

Source: *ECOTEC Research and Consulting Ltd.*

2

Nuclear energy versus coal

The greenhouse effect and acid rain have revived discussion that nuclear electricity generation will come back into fashion. Nuclear power stations produce no carbon dioxide or gases which cause acid rain, and seem preferable, on these grounds, to fossil fuels. Relative emissions of CO_2 from power stations are:

Coal	100
Oil	80
Gas	60
Nuclear	10
Hydro	10

Compare factors which might assist in making an ethical choice of energy sources. For example, there are reports that children of workers at nuclear plants are more liable to contract cancer.

3 Global challenges: ethical responses

The level of public awareness of green issues is high. A recent Mintel Report on green consumerism shows that among shoppers:

- 90% consider air, sea and river pollution to be 'fairly or very serious';
- 80% are worried about acid rain, nuclear waste and leaded petrol;

- 65% are worried over the use of chemicals in farming;
- 50% are aware of power station emissions, sewerage and CFCs;
- 33% think that commercial and domestic polluters should be heavily fined.

Recent United Kingdom studies indicate that the level of awareness about environment problems remains low among managers. In a recent survey conducted by consultants Peat Marwick McLintock, it emerged that 66% of employers and 72% of employees in Britain thought that there were no specific environmental issues relating to their own companies.

But many businesses and industries are now attempting to keep pace with a growing international interest in 'green' topics.

Code of practice

On 25 March 1989, the US supertanker *Exxon Valdez* hit a reef and discharged 300,000 barrels of oil into the Gulf of Alaska. On 1 April, Exxon sacked the captain for being drunk on duty. Exxon chiefs accepted liability at a Senate enquiry, which set the cost of cleaning the area at between $100 and $200 million. Environmental groups banded together with institutional investors to investigate ways of preventing such accidents. In Britain, attached to the Environment Protection Bill is a code which places a duty on industry to ensure that all waste is properly disposed of.

Corporate programmes

In the United Kingdom, a group of leading companies, including IBM, ICI, Costain, Tesco and British Telecom, has formed Business in the Environment to cooperate in taking action on environment problems.

Figure 13
Business in the Environment programme: helping managers to understand the commercial implications of environment

Government legislation

The UK government is putting through Parliament an Environment Protection Bill to tighten waste disposal regulations.

International cooperation

The twelve EC nations spent £28 billion on environmental control in 1987. This is expected to rise to £90 billion per annum in the early 1990s.

The United Nations' Environment Programme is playing a central role in securing international agreement on global warming.

Activities

1

Explain briefly the significance of the 15% 'green' vote in the European elections of 1989.

2

The Confederation of British Industry, the Royal Society for the Arts and the *Financial Times* promote the Better Environment Awards. Business is benefiting from the 'green' fashion. Is this a case of 'good business is good ethics'?

3

List five items in one of your local supermarkets labelled 'green' or with an ethical claim (such as 'free-range eggs'), and compare the price with similar non-green, non-ethical goods. Are 'green' goods more or less expensive?

Dilemma

Making the right decisions in the environmentally conscious 1990s will mean looking closely at different moral and technical objectives. There is no simple ethical 'rule of thumb': many factors have to be balanced out. Tackle these cases and try to offer ethical solutions:

1. A new baby has arrived in the family. You can:
   (a) take sides in the 'environment friendly' war between manufacturers

of disposable nappies – use them and add to the mountains of rubbish on our landscapes; or

(b) buy reusable cloth nappies which need regular washing, thus adding to the use of energy and the volume of detergents in rivers.

2. The local supermarket has introduced two new health drinks. You can choose either:

(a) the plastic packaged one, which is energy efficient to produce, but will add to the rubbish mountain; or

(b) the recyclable glass packaged one, which will involve you in trips to the bottle bank, leading, possibly, to increased energy use and exhaust emissions.

Unit 9 The World of Money

1 Intermediation

The world of money is an *intermediation* or a 'go-between' system. It is a business world in which financial institutions link individuals, other institutions and the world of work. Intermediation can be defined as 'the process by which income, spending, saving, financial surplus and investment are linked to the world of work and production' (see Figure 14).

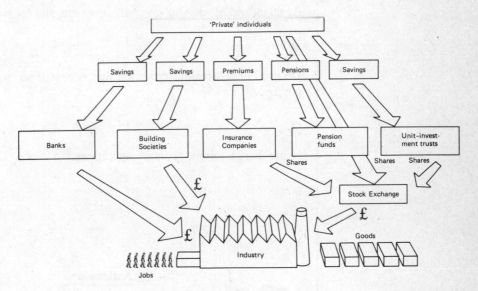

Figure 14
Intermediation

What emerges from this figure is that everyone is caught up in the world of money. It is not a vast, impersonal financial system. *Individuals* spend a lot of time and effort dealing with money. The *financial system* is worked by people and works to help people to make money for themselves and for others, as well as for national and for international institutions and trade. In Britain, *the City*, the square mile in London where financial services are concentrated, functions as the main financial sector of the UK economy.

Activities

The importance of money

Money is something we use to buy a pair of jeans, a Walkman or sportswear. Without it life would become very difficult. It is necessary, too, for the development of new technologies, for setting up industries and to enable trading to take place with other countries. It oils the wheels in the process of creating wealth and thereby contributes to the enjoyment of a higher standard of living.

Importance for *individuals*: 80% of the British population now saves regularly – on average, about 12% of disposable income. From the sale of houses left to them by their parents (who were pioneers of the 1950s property-owning democracy), they invest about £5 billion per year.

1

As an individual, do you save? If so, where and for what purpose?

2

Do you belong to an organisation that saves? If so, where and for what purpose?

3

Name five important financial institutions

i.
ii.
iii.
iv.
v.

Figure 15

The importance of *the City* can be understood from a number of factors: it provides capital markets for the allocation of funds; it offers effective payment services; it provides employment for 22,000 people; and it contributes to the balance of payments through invisible earnings, that is, money earned through the traditional British skills in dealing with investments, insurance and shipping insurance.

List any other City services you can discover:

2 Ethics and intermediation

Out of thirty practitioners from the world of money (bankers, stock exchange dealers, insurance brokers, pension fund managers etc.) almost every one identified two characteristics of their work: *service* and *effectiveness*. (Many of the details in this section can be found in a report, *Morals and Money*, prepared by the Research Unit at St John's College, Wonersh, Guildford, 1990.)

These characteristics provide the foundation for a *positive* ethic of money-taking and money-making. If service is honest and fair, it will evoke trust in the customers. At this point, bankers and stock exchange personnel recalled the motto of the City: *My Word is my Bond*. Financiers are not the 'baddies' of the world of business. They must make profits, or they fail; but their purpose is to assist the production of goods and services which others want. The beginning of business ethics in the City is the vision that those who work there are doing more than satisfying their own greed.

Customers trust both the honesty of financiers and their skill and expertise in taking risks with money in order to transform it into further earnings. The market at which financial institutions are looking to invest people's funds (to the advantage of both parties) is now a highly competitive one, as you can see from the financial pages of any newspaper. The customer lacks the expertise, but he has the money; and when he puts it with an institution, he, in some sense, becomes a *stakeholder*, and is, therefore, a co-creator of wealth. This has implications for the distribution of wealth. In the world of money, however, as one editor of the financial pages of a daily newspaper said when being interviewed, profit is seen as a pure return for exceptional skill, and it tends to include a reluctance to distribute.

3 Ethics and selected money problems

In both the public sector (where Government is the main employer) and in the private sector, there are a number of outstanding issues connected with money which call for serious ethical attention attention. It is impossible to deal with them all, but a few issues are selected below which point to problems which will be important in the 1990s, and show how they are ethical as well as business problems.

Taxes

It is easy to get the feeling that you are over-taxed! There is a tax on your wage packet, a tax on cigarettes, a tax on a drink when you go to the pub, a tax on petrol, a tax on profits which you earn from shares. And then there is the Poll Tax and Value Added Tax. The latter came in during

1979, and is 15% extra which we pay on goods and services, and which the shopkeeper passes on to the Inland Revenue.

The Government has five reasons for raising taxes:

1. to raise money for government;
2. to raise the prices and reduce the consumption of harmful products such as tobacco;
3. to transfer wealth from the rich to the poor;
4. to encourage the sale of home products by making foreign goods more expensive;
5. to dampen inflation by taking purchasing power out of the economy.

An important question to be asked is: What is a good tax? Adam Smith, the founding father of British economics, answered 200 years ago (and it is still a good answer) that taxes must be *fair* (taking account of ability to pay); must *not discourage* people from working; must be *cheap to collect*; and *easy to understand*.

Activities

1

Is the Poll Tax a good tax by the above standards?

2

One of the cheaper Scotch blended whiskies sells for £7 a bottle.
15% goes to VAT (91p);
63% goes to excise duty (£4.41);
3.5% goes to corporation tax (25p);
14% goes to costs (98p)
6.5% is net profit (45p).

Is this fair: ● to the consumer?
           ● to the manufacturer?
           ● to the government?

3

Value Added Tax is called a 'regressive' tax because it takes a larger proportion of a poor person's income. Is this fair on all buyers?

Acquisitions

The term 'acquisitions' covers all forms of mergers: takeovers; management buy-outs (MBOs, that is, when a company or part of it is bought by its existing management); management buy-ins (MBIs, that is, when management from outside buys a company or part of it). Acquisition activity has been at such a pitch in recent years that it has been referred to as 'merger mania'.

Takeovers are big business. In 1984 there were £270 million of buy-outs. In 1985 MBOs went up to £1 billion, and to almost £5 billion in 1988. MFI furniture was bought out for £714 million in 1988. Financial institutions earn large fees for their work in financing mergers, typically £1 million on every £200 million deal.

The ethical problems of takeovers are often concerned with advantage or damage to shareholders, whose interests are protected by the *City Code on Takeovers and Mergers*. The Code's professed objective is to ensure fair and equal treatment for all shareholders in relation to takeovers, since statistics show that the value of shares of the unsuccessful predator is usually depressed for years. The trouble is that shareholders have virtually no way of successfully challenging their company's acquisition strategy, and so can be put at a disadvantage by ambitious managers. Another ethical problem with takeovers is known as 'leverage buy-outs', where the prospective purchaser (sometimes referred to as 'predator', because there are hunters in this market) borrows money to support his purchase (this money is called 'junk bonds'), having worked out in advance that he will sell off parts of the company he is going to buy and end up with a much cheaper purchase. Borrowings are higher. In 1981, £50 was lent for every £100 the prospective purchaser had. By 1989, banks and lending institutions were lending £530 for every £100. The buying of companies was being financed by huge debts, though it must also be said (according to a survey published in November 1990) that UK buy-outs in the past decade provided a total employment of 600,000 and increased profits in many cases.

Activities

1

In 1989, Hoylake, bidding on behalf of Sir James Goldsmith, Lord Rothschild and Kerry Packer, tried to gain control of British and American Tobaccos. The bid failed. RIT capital Partners, an investment trust involved in the deal, showed a decline of almost £20 million in the value of its holding in Anglo Group. Shares in Anglo fell from 450p to 193p. Is it fair for shareholders to be vulnerable in this way?

> **2**
>
> In the last couple of years, companies sometimes set up an Employee Share-Ownership Plan (ESOP) at the time of arranging a buy-out. A trust is set up, which can buy shares and offer them, at 80% of market value, to employees once the buy-out is completed. Discuss whether or not this is management acting with fairness and respect, and therefore ethically.

Insider dealing

Mark, a sociologist employed to do a study of values in the City on behalf of a Corporate Responsibility and Business Ethics Consultancy, discovers in the course of his work that a move is underway for a buy-out of a large hotel chain by a US company. He buys a small amount of shares himself, and passes on the information to a business acquaintance in the City. Acting on this kind of price-sensitive information is insider dealing.

An insider dealer is "any person who, because of his employment or other confidential relationship with a public company, is in possession of particular information about the company not known to the ordinary shareholders of the company concerned, which, if known, would be likely substantially to affect the market price of such a company's securities," and who acts on this information or passes it on to others.

[Joint Statement of the Takeover Panel, 1973]

In Britain this is against the law and is regulated by the Company Securities (Insider Dealing) Act, 1985.

Activity

In November 1987, a US Insurance Company agreed to buy Minet Holdings. John Hales, a consultant, was called in by the executive vice-president of the Insurance Company to devise an incentive scheme to ensure that Minet senior executives would stay on after the takeover. Hales immediately bought 2,500 Minet shares at £3 each, and sold them three weeks later at £4.50, making a net profit of £3,415.

Did Hales act unethically when he took advantage of this price-sensitive information?

Top directors' pay and salaries

On the positive side, it can be said that differentials in salaries are justifiable on the grounds that skill and effectiveness should be rewarded. This point is made in the Institute of Directors' statement on Directors'

Pay (12 July 1989). But, on the negative side, the sheer magnitude of the gap between such salaries and the wages of the vast majority of the working population, and the size of increases at a time when wage rises are being limited in order to control inflation, calls for careful ethical scrutiny. Given the sense of success which directors enjoy, the cars and free private medical insurance which they have, as well as the job satisfaction, is there not, at least, a case for voluntary restraint?

Activities

1

Study the list which follows and write a short ethical comment.
Top directors' pay

Company (financial year ending)	Recipient	Salary (£)
Smith Kline and Beecham (12/89)	Chairman	1,998,000
Lazard Brothers & Co (12/89)	Chairman	1,562,959
Hanson (9/89)	Chairman	1,534,000
Lonrho (9/89)	Highest Paid Director	1,317,257
Manpower (10/89)	Chairman	1,082,000
BOC Group (9/89)	Chairman	937,390
Tilbury Group (12/89)	Highest Paid Director	902,000
Burton Group (9/89)	Chairman	899,000
Euromoney Publications (9/89)	Chairman	852,718
NM Rothschild (3/90)	Highest Paid Director	803,000
Barings (12/90)	Highest Paid Director	771,564
Daily Mail and General Trust (9/89)	Highest Paid Director	764,287
Midland Bank (12/89)	Highest Paid Director	725,844
TI Group (12/89)	Chairman	715,097
J Henry Schrod Wagg (12/89)	Highest Paid Director	709,000
British Petroleum (12/89)	Chairman	708,722
Glaxo Holdings (6/90)	Chairman	683,927
Ratners Group (2/90)	Chairman	664,303
Kingfisher (2/90)	Highest Paid Director	657,000
Ferranti International (3/90)	Chairman	646,000
Ladbroke Group (12/89)	Chairman	643,000
SG Warburg Group (3/90)	Highest Paid Director	639,000
WPP Group (12/89)	Highest Paid Directors	629,000
Samuel Montagu & Co (12/89)	Highest Paid Director	627,000
Cable & Wireless (3/90)	Chairman	626,947
Saatchi & Saatchi (9/89)	Chairman	625,000
Marks & Spencer (3/90)	Chairman	619,961
BNB Resources (12/89)	Highest Paid Director	608,370
BAT Industries (12/89)	Chairman	601,813

Berisford International (9/89)	Chairman	600,000
Williams Holdings (12/89)	Chairman	594,000
Morgan Grenfell (12/89)	Highest Paid Director	558,196
Tate & Lyle (9/89)	Chairman	534,000
Tiphook (4/90)	Chairman	532,000
Dixon's Group (4/90)	Chairman	526,693
British Airways (3/90)	Chairman	515,818
Brent Walker Group (12/89)	Chairman	515,000
ICI (12/89)	Chairman	514,000
Tomkins (4/90)	Highest Paid Director	513,000
Anglo Group (3/90)	Chairman	512,000
Kleinwort Benson Group (12/89)	Highest Paid Director	509,305
Robert Flemming Holdings (3/90)	Highest Paid Director	507,000
Grand Metropolitan (9/89)	Chairman	506,438

Source: Monks Partnership Limited, Saffron Waldon, Essex.

2

Discuss the following quote:

"It is as if the enterprise culture, yuppydom, enormous salaries etc., – having given as much wealth as the market can give – has not addressed the question: What do I do with this wealth

- for myself?
- for my time?
- for the people I come into contact with?
- for the world around me?

This is the real dilemma of our times."

[Norman Strauss, BBC Discussion, 'Washes Whiter', 28 April 1990]

Ethical investment

In recent years, ethical investment has attracted serious notice in Britain. In 1989, the Ethical Investment Research and Information Service (established in 1983) listed 14 ethical funds run by 12 enterprises. Two important national institutions, the Law Society and the National Trust, have shown interest in such funds.

Ethical investment involves using funds not only for profit but also in keeping with two other principles: obedience to the law; and obedience to certain specific ethical guidelines. These guidelines are as follows:

- Certain goods may be inherently bad and should not be encouraged (armaments, tobacco).
- The process of production may be unacceptable, for example, animal experimentation.

- The location of production may be undesirable, as for instance, in a country under a tyrannical regime.
- Marketing methods may be of doubtful status, for example, dishonest advertising.
- The distribution of funds may be questionable, if, for instance, they are channelled to certain political funds or to bodies.

For information on ethical investment, write to:

EIRIS Services Limited, Bondway Business Service,
71 Bondway, London, SW8 1SQ.

PIRC, 40 Bowling Green Lane, LONDON, EC1R 0NE.

On 'green' funds, write to:

Merlin Jupiter Unit Trust Management, Knightsbridge House, 197 Knightsbridge, London, SW7 1RB.

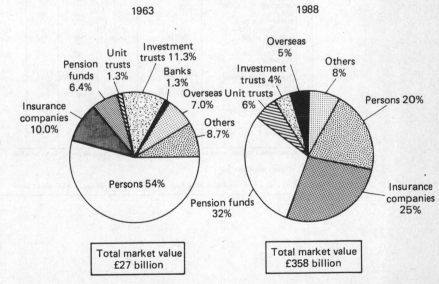

Figure 16
Pattern of share ownership

Activities

1

Study the information given in Figure 16, and compare different funds. If you were investing money, where would you put it? Give your reasons.

Keywords

In your own words, write down what is meant by the following, explaining also the ethical aspects of the words:

Mediation　　　　　*Risk management*　　　*Risk transformation*
Acquisitions　　　　*Ethical funds*　　　　*Green Funds*
Insider information　*Stakeholders*

2

Write an essay on the ethical implications of the following table:

Investment with a conscience

Fund	Performance since launch	Total SRI funds (£m)	Geographical spread	Outside specialist	Independent committee	Products available		
						Unit trust	Pension	Pep
Friends Provident Stewardship (Eth & Env)	25/99 (5 yrs)*	£158m	UK/N Amer	Yes	Yes	Yes	Yes	Yes
Credit Suisse Buckmaster Moore Fellowship (Eth)	57/110 (3 yrs)	£6m	Int	Yes	Yes	Yes	Yes	Yes
Medical Investments Health (Eth & Env)	120/141 (2 yrs)	£0.75m	Int	No	Yes	Yes	No	No
Abbey Life Ethical (Eth & Env)	42/150 (2 yrs)	£7m	Mainly UK	No	Yes	Yes	Yes	No
NM Conscience (Eth & Env)	70/180 (2 yrs)	£9m	Mainly UK	No	Yes	Yes	Yes	Yes
Target Life Global Opportunities (Eth & Env)	92/141 (2 yrs)	£7.8m	Int	No	Yes	Yes	Yes	No
Allchurches Life Annuity (Eth & Env)	9/180 (2 yrs)	£6m	UK	No	Yes	Yes	Yes	No
Merlin Ecology (Eth & Env)	51/141 (2 yrs)	£32.6m	Int	No	Yes	Yes	No	No
Scott Equit Ethical Pension (Eth)	131/141 (1 yr)	£4.2m	UK	Yes	Yes	Yes	Yes	No
Acorn Ethical Unit (Eth & Env)	89/152 (1 yr)	£0.5m	Int	No	No	Yes	No	No
Sovereign Ethical (Eth)	11/208 (6 mths)	£2.7m	UK	No	Yes	Yes	No	Yes
Eagle Star Environmental Opportunities (Env)	5/208 (6 mths)	£5.5m	Mainly UK	No	No	Yes	No	Yes
TSB Environmtal Investor (Env)	69/208 (6 mths)	£13.7m	Mainly UK	Yes	Yes	Yes	Yes	Yes
CU Environmtal Exempt Pension (Env)	N/A	£4.9m	Int	No	No	No	Yes	No
Clerical Medical Evergreen (Env)	N/A	£3.8m	Int	Yes	No	Yes	Yes	No

Source: Holden Meehan, independent insurance consultants. Report available free of charge from Bristol office. Tel: 0272 252874.

* Denotes period since launch.

(Eth) denotes funds investing on ethical basis: (Env) denotes those investing on environmental basis.

Unit 10 | Fraud, Regulation and Business Ethics

1 The growth of fraud

Public awareness of fraud has grown in recent years. In general, commercial fraud covers a multitude of sins such as: obtaining credit without intending to pay; obtaining money through mail-order business without delivering the goods; obtaining money with promises to invest it and not doing so; obtaining money by computer fraud; and insider dealing. It becomes 'corporate crime' when business people deceive other businesses or the tax authorities or investors.

In the ten years between 1977 and 1987 the number of offenders cautioned for fraud and forgery in Britain grew from 1,500 to 3,900. The number of fraud and forgery cases recorded by the police in 1980 was 105,200, and by 1987 it had risen to 133,000. The City in particular has proved to be a fertile ground for headline-hitting fraud and alleged fraud cases: Barlow Clowes, Guinness and Blue Arrow are notable examples. The Roskill Report estimated that fraud in the City was in danger of running at around £3 billion. The City police fraud squad reckons that City interests committed frauds amounting to £500 million in the first half of 1989.

Amount of fraud dealt with by City of London Fraud Squad (in £m)

1980	54
1981	54
1982	100
1983	115
1984	302
1985	482

2 Tackling fraud

By the early 1980s, the Government was being pressed to deal with the growing incidence of fraud. In that year, the Fraud Investigation Group was set up to impose some order on attempts to investigate fraud and to deal with it. Although it brought the Director of Public Prosecutions, the police and trade department officials together, the FIG proved to be ineffective. It did, however, influence the establishment, in 1983, of the Roskill Committee on fraud, which published its report in 1986. Its main conclusions were:

i. Changes in the law would not be enough: the investigating authorities and the courts needed to change their attitudes.
ii. Trial by jury should be replaced by a fraud trials tribunal.
iii. More resources must be made available.

The Government has ruled out the recommendation that juries be replaced by fraud tribunals. The complexities of commercial fraud, however, are such that judge and jury may not understand them. In Germany, judges have to undertake special university courses in order to qualify for fraud trials. Should we adopt this system?

A main result of the Roskill Report was the setting up of the Serious Fraud Office (SFO) by the 1987 Criminal Justice Act. It is accountable to the Attorney General and to Parliament. Its aims are as follows:

• to develop a coherent approach to the investigation of serious fraud;
• to speed up investigation and institute criminal proceedings;
• to develop expertise in particular areas, such as the Stock Exchange;
• to present evidence effectively and comprehensibly;
• to increase the proportion of successful prosecutions.

Other enforcement agents include the Department of Trade, the Inland Revenue, the Department of Social Security and, increasingly, the City's self-regulating organisations (SROs). All this is part of the apparatus of ethics for controlling fraudulent practices.

Dilemma

Dealing with fraud costs a lot and does great harm to individuals. Yet, a tolerant view is taken of it. A recent writer has said: ". . . Persistent offenders who steal £1 go to prison; persistent insider dealers who steal £10 million pay back the money – perhaps in addition to a substantial fine; on the rare occasion that they are caught. *De maximis non curat lex*: for the greatest offences the law has no care."

(Levi, M., *Regulating Fraud: White-Collar Crime and the Criminal Process*, Tavistock Publications, London, 1987).

Activity

Reasons for the tolerant attitude towards fraud include:

(a) It is not a violent crime.
(b) The victim is often wealthy or an institution, and can afford it.
(c) The offender is often of good standing in society.

Add some further reasons to this list.

3 Regulating the City

In the late 1980s, the Serious Fraud Office established contact with the Securities and Investment Board, which had been set up in 1986 by the Financial Services Act. Along with the traditional system for regulating the banking world and money markets, the SFO and the new regulatory structure, of which the SIB is a central element, provide an apparatus for controlling the world of money and its lapses and excesses. This should go some way to achieving what the Governor of the Bank of England, in a recent speech, identified as the need for "all business in the City of London – of whatever type – to be guided by the highest professional and ethical standards."

Activity

Study figures 17 and 18 (both on page 66), and go on from there to investigate what kinds of control the various SROs exercise. Further information can be obtained from the Securities and Investment Board, 3 Royal Exchange Buildings, LONDON, EC3V 3NL.

4 Codes of ethics

The law, the Serious Fraud Office, the Department of Trade and the new regulatory structure are attempts to secure legal compliance and sound practice by external coercion. But from inside the business constituency itself there are growing attempts to control lapses and to encourage positive ethical practice by devising Codes of Business Ethics, Codes of Practice, Professional Codes of Conduct, and Corporation Credos. One advantage of such codes is that they assist companies to think through a corporation philosophy. And given the consensus nature of modern business, influential codes are a useful addition to legal and coercive measures.

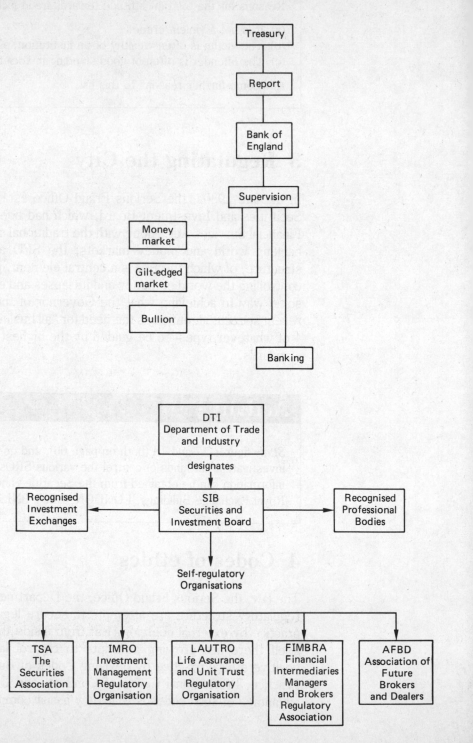

Figure 17
Regulating banking

Figure 18
*The new regulatory
structure*

There are a number of influential international codes:

OECD Code: The Organization for Economic Cooperation and Development issued intergovernmental guidelines for multinational companies: *Declaration on international investment and multinational enterprises*. The Code offers guidelines for multinational corporations in their investment policies and relations with the host government.

ILO Code: *Tripartite declaration concerning multinational enterprises and social policy*, promulgated by the International Labour Organization, is mainly concerned with employment and social elements in the involvement of multinational corporations.

ICC Code: *International code of fair treatment for foreign investments* sets standards for fair treatment in foreign investments, both for individual investors and for home and host governments.

In Britain there is a steady growth of companies, organisations and professional bodies which are now devising codes of ethics for themselves. Here are a few examples:

British Institute of Management: Code of conduct with supporting guides to good management practice. The Code requires members to uphold the good standing of BIM, complying with the law and respecting customs of any country in which business is conducted. Managers are held to high standards of efficiency and responsibility in respect of suppliers and customers. Bribery is outlawed.

British Telecom: Solving problems: code of practice. The Code sets out details on the kind of service that BT offers, recourse on query of bills, and entitlement to repairs and complaints procedures.

Activities

1

Find examples of Codes of Business Ethics or Practice. The Institute of Business Ethics, 12 Palace Street, LONDON, SW1E 8JA, will help.

2

Join with your class group in constructing a code of ethics for a business of your choice. The code should cover three areas:
(a) The purpose of the organisation and its aims and values. *What kind of* organisation is it?
(b) What are the rules on which it runs? *How* is it going to become a certain kind of organisation?
(c) Rules for daily practice. *What* is to be done?

3

Study the British Telecom *Code of Practice for Consumers*, to be found at the back of every telephone directory, and suggest additions or improvements.

5 Ethics and employee fraud

Fraud is not a matter just for employers, business and professional people. It is widespread and exists in many forms throughout the world of work. A survey of 2,058 adults, conducted by MORI in 1985, gives some idea of the range of offences and attitudes to them. The table below summarises the findings:

Offence	Thinking morally wrong %	Thinking generally acceptable to most people %	Knowing someone else doing %	Admitting having done themselves %
Paying someone in cash who doesn't charge VAT	30	49	25	14
Accepting cash for some work in order to keep earnings free of VAT or income tax	35	37	20	7
Using an employer's telephone without permission	36	35	26	20

Paying cash to someone if you suspect he or she isn't paying income tax	41	33	20	8
Taking time off when you're supposed to be at work	66	21	28	11
People on the dole earning some money without telling the social-security office	67	24	32	3
Claiming expenses from an employer to which you are not entitled	70	16	18	4
Taking home things from work without paying for them	72	19	25	10
None of these	4	9	16	36
All eight of these	16	4	8	1

Source: adapted from MORI poll, conducted for the *Sunday Times*, October 1985.

Activities

1

Study the table and write a short account of your findings.

2

Discuss the view that what the law and external coercion does not achieve, must be left to business ethics.

Unit 11 Credit and Debt

1 Credit and debt

It is worth emphasising the difference between these two situations. *Credit* allows us to enjoy the benefits of goods and services before we have even paid for them. It is a common and useful system of buying and selling. Over half the homes bought in Britain are bought on credit (that is, with the help of a mortgage); and once people have moved into these homes they take their electricity and gas and telephones on credit; that is, they settle up after using the facilities. Strictly speaking, credit becomes *debt* only if you fail to pay the bills on time. But from the point of view of consumers, it is more realistic to regard any money owed to others as debt, since it needs taking into account when spending income.

There are many types of credit, and, therefore, many types of potential debt. Here is a list:

Hire purchase (the goods belong to you only when you have made the final payment)
Credit sale   (like HP, but you own the goods immediately)
Credit cards
Charge cards
Store cards
Bank loans
Building Society loans
Finance Company loans
Mail order catalogues
Pawnbroking
Small money lenders

Figure 19

Activities

1

From magazines, newspapers and mail order catalogues, make a collection of credit advertisements; pick up a selection of leaflets on credit from shops and banks. Classify them according to the above list.

2

Write to the Office of Fair Trade for information on *Credit* and *Debt*.

Sources of debt

A recent survey of 1,000 people with debt problems showed that there are four main credit sources among those listed above. The average amounts of money owed are also given:

Finance companies	£2,758
Banks	£1,789
Credit cards	£1,021
Stores	£ 725

Most of these debts began their life in credit advertising which asked consumers to spend money which has not yet been earned.

2 Growth of personal debt

Personal debt has grown enormously in Britain: it has doubled since 1983. A recent estimate of current personal debt puts it at £40 billion in the whole of the United Kingdom, which means an average of £1,800 debt per household. Perhaps the most common reaction to such figures is that debt is incurred mainly by the feckless and irresponsible; but a detailed survey of people in debt, conducted by the Jubilee Centre in Cambridge, shows that it affects all classes in society and all income groupings. This survey (as well as other studies) points to the likelihood of other factors, since young people with several dependent children and single-parent families are over-represented in the samples of people in debt. A survey conducted by the Office of Population Censuses and Surveys in 1981 found that 11% of debtor households contained four or more dependent children. The Jubilee Centre Survey, conducted in 1986, found that a sample of 1,043 cases of debt included 1,167 children. Debt is a family problem.

Activity

Study the table and histogram shown below and work out possible reasons for getting into debt.

Distribution of household types within sample and nationally

Household Type	Percentage of sample (1)	Percentage of national population (2)
Married/cohabiting couple with no children	17	35
Married/cohabiting couple with 1 or 2 children	34	24
Married/cohabiting couple with 3 or more children	11	5
Lone parent with 1 or more children	13	4
Other	26	32

Sources: (1) *Jubilee Centre Debt Study Survey.*
(2) *1985 General Household Survey* (OPCS), quoted in *Social Trends 17,* Table 2.1, p.41 (HMSO).

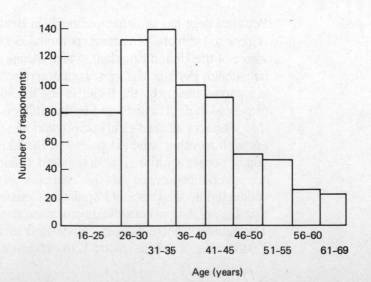

Figure 20
Histogram showing age distribution of respondents

3 The human and ethical consequences

Out of one million enquiries registered for help at London's Citizens Advice Bureaux last year, 20% were about debt. 200,000 people, and, in many cases, their families, found themselves in trouble on account of debt. The human and moral consequences of such debts are well documented:

(a) *Mental problems:* depression and worry. In addition to the personal effects, this also restricts the efficiency of people at work, and is sometimes the cause of accidents.
(b) *Social withdrawal:* debt involves a loss of freedom, and has adverse effects on people's social lives.
(c) *Physical ailments:* the general psychosomatic results (that is, the mind affecting the body) are well documented, and the damage to health is sometimes of a serious nature.
(d) *Marital problems:* in an in-depth study of 50 individuals, fourteen said that they had experienced serious marriage difficulties connected with debt. This finding is supported by evidence from marriage advisory councils.
(e) *Family problems:* family breakdown occurs as a result of debt, often because parents feel a sense of guilt that they cannot buy things for their children. The children themselves are often quiet and withdrawn, showing signs of social withdrawal also. They frequently do less well at school.

It is evident that the consequences of debt are a mixture of personal and social elements. There are other less obvious consequences, too, such as that income which goes to service debt contributes to the restriction of economic growth. Most general of all, the debt mentality becomes part of the ethos of the society and encourages irresponsible borrowing, greed and the temptation to crookedness.

The final outcome is sometimes dramatic: debt leads to court action for recovery. In Britain there are 2 million such cases every year, of which about 1 million are cases taken out by firms against individuals.

Activity

Draw up lists of the personal and social consequences of debt, and then explain the ways in which they are ethical or moral problems:

Personal   *Social*

4 Ethical responsibilities of the borrower

From the point of view of the consumer, the greatest temptation is convenience, the ultimate form of which is the ability to buy goods which could not be afforded if they had to be paid for on the spot. The temptation is ever present: if you walk down the street there are notices offering anything from £200 to £2,000 for 'instant' spending. No need to save. No need to do without. The item you want can be yours immediately.

Purchase by credit is dressed up attractively. It saves the trouble of carrying a cheque book; it is said to allow you 'to spread the costs'; it confers spending power.

Activities

Work out the advantages and disadvantages of the 'spending power' made available in the following example:

A store runs a continuous credit scheme into which you pay £30 per month and which entitles you to draw goods to the value of £720 (24 times your monthly repayment). If the interest on your credit (remember this is really your *debt*) is 2.4% per month, the record of your buying could look like this over a 4-month period:

Date	Item	Credit/debt	Balance
1 Jan	Credit	£30.00	£30.00
4 Jan	Jeans & blouses	£89.90	
25 Jan	Sweater	£21.95	
1 Feb	Credit	£30.00	£51.85
11 Feb	Underwear	£27.29	
	Jewellery	£14.95	
	Shoes	£35.00	
27 Feb	Coat	£110.00	
28 Feb	Interest	£1.24	
1 Mar	Credit	£30.00	£159.09
10 Mar	Dress	£66.95	
	Skirt	£44.50	
	Tights	£3.00	
20 Mar	Blouse	£19.95	
31 Mar	Interest	£3.82	
1 April	Credit	£30.00	£257.31

1

Write a comment in which you compare the privilege of 'spreading the cost' with the interest you will have to pay on these purchases over a year.

2

"The credit card is a risky status symbol." Discuss.

5 Ethical responsibilities of the lender

In their advertising, banks, finance houses and other credit institutions resemble fairy godmothers. But they are not. By granting personal loans, banks and finance houses make a profit on the interest you pay. By giving credit cards they gain not only from the interest, but also by taking a cut from the retailer's profit on the transactions.

There is a credit boom (and a debt mountain) because:

(a) it is profitable;
(b) it is competitive;
(c) it is possible, in the sense that credit cards and automated technology make it feasible to keep track of millions of such accounts.

But since credit can so easily turn into unmanageable debt, it is partly the responsibility of lenders to make sure that new technology and marketing methods do not make the borrower the slave of the lender. There can be sophisticated profiteers as well as loansharks in this market.

In one survey, 17% of those interviewed said that easy credit is a factor in over-indebtedness. In the UK as a whole, there was a greater than 10% growth in consumer credit in the 1980s, which is attributable, in part, to the fashion of willingness to be in debt, on the borrowing side, and to pressure promotion in a competitive market. Thus, between 1982 and 1986, expenditure on TV advertising of credit cards rose from £9.3m to £16.7m. The recent *Monopolies and Mergers Commission report on credit card activities* (September 1989) criticised companies for profiteering through the operation of an unofficial cartel to keep interest rates high. "Since 1979" writes the report, "on average, bank credit card interest has been 14% higher than the bank base rate, and more often than not, double it. This is impossible to justify."

Another ethical problem can arise with the Annual Percentage Rate (APR). Borrowing is expensive. Here Government legislation is helpful, since all organisations are required by law to state the total amount they charge for credit. This figure is represented by the APR. This is difficult to calculate, and rates vary greatly. It pays to shop around and, if you do not understand, to take advice. The onus is on the consumer.

Activities

1

Look at Figure 21 and write a short comment on 'the cost of borrowing'.

2

Only 0.1% of credit is devoted to debt education. Is this a serious response to a massive social problem?

3

Organise a 'debt education seminar' in your college or school.
The Jubilee Centre, Jubilee House, 3 Hooper Street, Cambridge, CB1 2NZ, will help with video and study pack material.

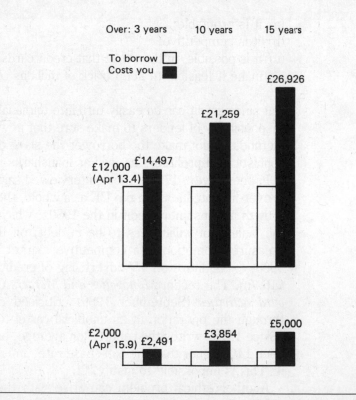

Figure 21
The cost of borrowing

Unit 12 Using Ethical Reasoning

1 The difficulty of ethical decisions

Making moral or ethical decisions is always difficult. In recent years, committees have sat for months discussing whether research should be permitted on human embryos at all, or whether it should, perhaps, be permitted but only up to 14 days of embryonic existence. When it was debated in Parliament, the Prime Minister and an Archbishop, both with a scientific background, voted in favour of allowing such experimentation up to 14 days. There have been similar debates about whether abortion should be allowed up to 18 weeks, or 21 weeks, or even 28 weeks. Again, opinion has been divided.

If there is difficulty in arriving at moral decisions in personal matters, there is even more in corporate matters. Business is dynamic, competitive, changing and complex; and trying to find principles which can provide guidance in all circumstances is a tall order. Furthermore, some people in business think they can draw a veil over personal ethics and conscience when they leave for work in the morning. If some action looks dubious, they say: 'It's the job', 'Everybody does it', 'That's the way the City works', or 'If the boss asks you, do it'. Even those with a private morality often separate it from corporate morality.

What business needs is a set of guidelines for thinking about ethics. The guidelines should help directors, managers and employees to:

(a) identify the *nature* of ethical problems; and
(b) *decide* which course of action is ethical in each particular situation.

Here is a checklist for conducting an ethics test:
(1) Facts *do not* dictate values: what **is** never fully defines what **ought to be**.
(2) Not all choices are simply between good and evil. Sometimes the choice is between two courses which are good, but one of which is more desirable for particular reasons. At other times, good and evil exist simultaneously in lines of action available to a manager.
(3) Knowledge of consequences is limited.
(4) Management is often dealing with several different constituents, each of which has its own ethical claims.

(5) Different individuals and groups inside the corporation have their own ethical stances.
(6) Ethical standards vary over time and place.
(7) Ethical principles are difficult to bring down to particular cases.
(8) New technology, statistical methods and scientific understanding make ethical decisions more remote.
(9) Multinational organisations, with different cultural locations, limit the unity of opinion which assists the acceptance of ethical decisions.

Here are nine examples of each of the above. Provide another example of each:

(1) A company decides to invest in South African diamonds because all available information says that this is a profitable investment. But the apartheid policy of the mining company may be a reason for saying it ought not to be used.

   Your example . . . .

(2) Your firm is located in the inner city where most of the population is black, but only 15% of your workforce is black. The workforce you have is well trained, and taking on black workers is going to involve extra costs. But fairness to the community must be considered as grounds for looking at your employment practices. Perhaps there should be positive discrimination in favour of more black workers.

   Your example . . . .

(3) Your company sells pharmaceuticals in an overseas country, and you do not foresee that the product may be misused with serious health consequences. What do you do when such evidence begins to emerge?

   Your example . . . .

(4) The customer requires speedy delivery, but the stress caused to the workforce by pressure practices is great. Which do you choose?

   Your example . . . .

(5) Your pharmaceutical company produces drugs which have an abortion-inducing effect. Some strict Catholics, who are excellent workers from every other point of view, do not want to be involved in the production of this particular product. Do you dismiss them?

   Your example . . . .

(6) At one time, when your company traded only in England, you would never have considered any form of bribery. But now you are dealing with a number of Third World companies where bribery seems to be an accepted part of business life. If you do not engage in the practice, you get no contracts. What do you do?

Your example . . . .

(7) You accept the general principle that nuclear war is immoral, but you work in a nuclear research establishment. Your work is supposed to be applied to peaceful uses of nuclear energy; but you are aware that it has got military potential. Are you bound to give up your job in defence of your principles?

Your example . . . .

(8) You work in a firm of brokers, where computers have made information technology have such instantaneous results that the human factor in making moral decisions does not have time to come into play. Do you simply take the line that there is nothing you can do about it?

Your example . . . .

(9) You are a director of a multinational oil company, with operations in Britain, USA, Mexico and Saudi Arabia. You find it difficult to have a Code of Ethics accepted because you are dealing with Christians, Muslims and secular mentalities. Do you have three codes?

Your example . . . .

2 Making ethical connections

Many aspects of modern society which seem separate can actually be connected. In fact, our ethics will be superficial, applicable only to the case and not getting to grips with the forces and tendencies which shape our society, unless we recognise this.

For example, three sets of problems which seem to be separate are actually linked. Firstly, abortion, euthanasia and genetic engineering show a tendency towards the devaluation of persons. Secondly, consumerism diverts attention from human values and relationships of which we say that 'there is more to life than money'. Thirdly, the separation of the private and public spheres effects a split between the world of individuals and political and corporate life, and between personal and corporate morality. But lying behind all these trends is the force of technology and its tendency to make persons and human freedom less significant than scientific achievement and control.

Ethics must always look to the interplay between facts and their human consequences. It must seek to understand the forces and tendencies in society or corporations, and to face these with general principles. These are like signposts offering guidance through the ethical maze.

Activity

The local polytechnic is now including 'business ethics' in its Business Studies Course. The course is in four parts:

1. Are you proud to be in business?
2. The responsible company.
3. Communications: keeping in touch at all levels.
4. Business ethics: developing a code.

What do you think of this outline? Have you any suggestions to make?

3 Some ethical schemes

The following methods of ethical reasoning can be used for general guidance:

Method	Critical determining factors	An action is ethical when . . .	Limitations
Machiavellian	Ends justify means	Supports the ends of political power	It tolerates lies, breaking promises etc., as long as these achieve the desired end
Utilitarian (John Stuart Mill)	Comparing costs and benefits, inputs and outputs	Maximises pleasure	Difficult to quantify pleasure; does not settle which pleasures of what groups must be chosen

Categoric imperative (Kant)	People are ends in themselves	People are treated as ends in themselves and not as means	Difficult to validate
Rights under the law (Thomas Aquinas)	Respecting human rights	When life, liberty, the pursuit of happiness and 'economic rights' are secured	Difficult to balance conflicting rights
Establishing justice (Aristotle)	Finding a basic natural law	When there is proportionate distribution of the goods of the earth	Tends to be an abstract, universal and absolute theory not easily applicable to businesses

Activity

Choose a method that suits you and give reasons for your choice.

4 Applying ethical theory

Business ethics is an applied discipline. If it does not help people in business to make moral decisions, it may be fascinating but it is not useful. Whatever general theory is chosen to guide thinking on choices and decisions in business, it will be necessary to go through four stages, two of which are *descriptive* and two *prescriptive*, that is, two stages set out *what* the situation is, and the other two give guidance on *why* a particular course of action is preferable. Making ethical decisions is not easy: research and hard work are required in order to clarify and describe real situations (descriptive) so as to be able to set down rules and values ('normative', from 'norm', meaning 'a rule') which demands behaviour that goes beyond description. The stages are as follows:

Descriptive approaches	*Prescriptive approaches*
Scientific studies	General normative ethics
Conceptual studies	Applied normative ethics

Activity

Here is a list of excuses for doing nothing about business ethics or company responsibility, or moral dilemmas, or wrong business practices or . . . Many were given by managers in answers during the survey mentioned in Unit 2, section 1.

- Life is difficult enough in business already.
- This needs careful study before we take it on board.
- Religion and politics should not come into business.
- We are doing all that already.
- Those who want ethics can go to church.
- More money for more experts and advice.
- I agree in principle, but it is not practical.
- Don't try to find answers where there aren't any.

Reply to these objections.

For information on businesses, business ethics, social concerns of business and rules and regulations, the following bodies may be contacted:

The Stock Exchange, London, EC2N 1HP [071–588–2355]
The Stock Exchange, Scotland: Stock Exchange House, PO Box 141, Glasgow, G2 1BU [041–221–7060]
The Securities Association: The Stock Exchange, London, EC2N 1EQ [071–256–9000]
The Bank of England: Threadneedle Street, London, EC2R 8AH [071–601–4444]
Confederation of British Industry: 103 New Oxford Street, London, WC1A 1DU [071–379–7400]
The Institute of Directors: 116 Pall Mall, London, SW1Y 5ED [071–839–1233]
Securities and Investment Board: 3 Royal Exchange Buildings, London, EC3V 3NL [071–283–2474]
Insurance Brokers' Registration Council: 15 St Helen's Place, London, EC3A 6DS [071–588–4387]

Law Society: 113 Chancery Lane, London, WC2A 1PL [071–242–1222]

Industrial Common Ownership Movement: Corn Exchange, Leeds [0532–461737]

ESOP: Employee Share Ownership Plan: 1 Carlisle Avenue, London, EC3N 2ES [071–265–1147]

Ethical Investment Research Service: Bondway Business Centre, 71 Bondway, London, SW8 [071–735–1351]

Pensions Investment Research Consultants: 40 Bowling Green Lane, London, EC1R 0NE [071–833–4432]

The Ethical Investment Fund: D J Bromige & Partners, 10 Queen Street, Mayfair, London, W1X 7PD [071–491–0558]

Friends of the Earth: 377 City Road, London, EC1V 1NA [071–837–0731]

Green Peace UK: 30–31 Islington Green, London, N1 8XE [071–354–5100]

London Search Room: Companies House, 55–71 City Road, London, EC1Y 1BB [071–253–9393]

Institute of Business Ethics: 12 Palace Street, London, SW1E 8JA [071–931–0495]

Business Ethics Research Centre: King's College, London, WC2R 2LS [071–573–2510]

Business in the Community: 227a City Road, London, EC1U 1LX [071–253–3716]

A full listing of literature, institutions and other sources of information on Business Ethics can be found in:

McHugh, F. P., *Business Ethics: Keyguide to Information Sources* (London: Mansell, 1988).

Index